THE SACRIFICE

BY

RICHARD CRANE

PREFACE

The young girl finally found the book she had been looking for. The library had been out of it for weeks and she yearned to read it. She was a dreamer. She loved to read historical stories of other places including the lifestyles they had. It gave her an escape from her true-life boredom. She was not interested in fantasy or science fiction but explored the true historical literature that only came from living in those places. Biographies were her second favorite for it gave her the ability to live in that person's place, a different life than her own.

Finding a table in the far corner of the back room, she sat down and eagerly flipped open the book to read. .....

"The United Nations was always a leader. They led in industry, medical advancement and technology. They always helped other countries achieve freedom through means of negotiations and trading. Many smaller countries saw the United Nations as big bullies forcing their beliefs on others. Those countries would try to damage the UN's reputation by performing terrorist acts which caused the deaths of many innocent people. The United Nations also was a strong leader in weapons and if necessary, would use force to control barbaric leaders or organizations. The first chapters will break down the years and wars that the United Nations were involved in.

The largest contribution that the United Nations gave to the planet was technology. Ever since the disintegration of the ozone layer, the UN put all its efforts into a system that could reproduce ozone and resupply the planet. Many factories were built across the world. These installations were run by the top scientists of many countries and held at the top of the priority list. The second part of this book will cover the details of the process of these factories.

The last part of the book will deal with the medical breakthroughs that the United Nations have achieved. Cancer, which was one of the strongest killers among people, now has become almost nonexistent. Other medical technologies have greatly enhanced the human immune system and the common flu is a thing of the past. Many of...."

The girl's attention was broken by the ringing of a bell signifying that the library would close soon. She picked up the book and took it to the counter to check it out. The librarian stamped her reading card with a return date and the girl soon found herself running home, eager to continue her reading.

CHAPTER 1

Negotiations failed. Earth was in chaos. A terrorist organization called 'The Davi' had been causing many deaths not only in the United Nations but throughout the Middle East. For years the main control capitol of the Davi was hidden from view. It was never located in one place and seemed to move easily to a new area. The leader was never known but his staff would design and carry out actions that the world would call, 'Terror Traps', and nobody was safe from them. In the past year and a half, approximately 15,000 people had died in connections with Terror Traps.

In the past few weeks, though, combined forces had managed to corner the main Davi group in Egypt. Intelligence had discovered that not only did they have the Terror designers trapped but their leader as well. Several outer atmosphere fighter jets, armed satellites and Air stealth's were covering all borders. They had the group cornered in the mountains and satellite projectors showed that the terrorist was trapped. The world powers were ready to make their move and put an end to this group of killers.

The United Nations top technology station was well hidden. In an old abandoned barn was a crawl space that led to an elevator shaft. The elevator led down to a compound built a half a mile below the surface. The compound is surrounded by ten feet of lead and contains a jamming device that can block off all attempts of scanning. The base is the size of an average grocery store and has six men stationed in it. A Lieutenant Colonel and five enlisted men maintain its operations. The men are totally shut off from the world, except for the information they received from the Zenith Eclectic Universal System, commonly known as ZEUS. If the men want any news from home, they simply ask ZEUS. ZEUS was the main receiver, interpreter and strategic interceptor of all the United

Nations' systems. Any information that was assimilated by ZEUS, the six men was the first to know. The system also is the main control base for the entire network. Everything is connected to ZEUS.

The day started off as usual. Lieutenant Colonel Brent was enjoying a cup of coffee while sitting in his office reading the morning reports. Today's flavor was vanilla hazelnut for he could never drink straight black coffee and always added a flavor cream to the mix. For some reason the pumpkin spice didn't appeal to him even though it was the season for it. Butter pecan was his favorite but the supply room was out and wouldn't receive another shipment for three weeks. The coffee was his way of drifting away from the everyday problems of a commanding officer. When he combined the aroma, the taste and the warmth of the liquid going down his throat; it soothed the soul. It was, in fact, his way to meditate.

But things needed to be done and he shook his head to snap himself out of his trance and to get back to work. Going through the reports, he started assigning the daily tasks to the crew. No need to assign anything to Sergeant Jones for he was the cook and needed no direction. Brent did make a note to himself to review next month's menu to order supplies. The crew ate the best of what was offered and had the facilities to hold it. Crab, lobster and steak were always available but most of the crew favored hamburgers and bratwurst. They all enjoyed a well-cooked steak. No vegetarians were assigned to the compound.

Sergeants Bratton and Chenski were responsible for all repairs in the facility and had already started on the list handed to them last night after dinner. They both could build anything with only toothpicks to use and make it work. They were vain and at times it was hard to carry on a conversation with both of them in the same room. In fact, both tried to outdo each other all the time. Results were always a finished product that worked better than needed. When they worked together though, they were the best, which explained why they were attached to this facility.

Doctor Anthony was the medical officer and he had already handed him a list of upcoming physicals. Bratton was the only one on the list and needed to be done by the end of the week. He also received the medical inventory and needed to enter its contents into his report. The doctor was well trained and experienced not only in family practice but surgery as well. Outside of Bratton's broken arm, the facility never really had any emergencies. Cuts and burns were the only problems so far.

The last two officers stationed on the base were Sergeant's Brooks and Powell. They were the only personal, beside himself, that were allowed to enter ZEUS' operating room. They were nicknamed 'The Spooks' because everyone else rarely saw them. They would get up early, eat, and enter the control center and not be seen again until they handed their daily report in just before dinner. Usually at least ten pages long, it took most of the morning for Brent to sift through it and enter it into his report. Last night's report was seventeen pages, which is why he was planning on drinking a lot of coffee. It gave him more meditation for the mind.

According to last night's report, the combined forces had the enemy cornered in the mountains and were going to strike today with a new concept bomb called, 'The Dragon'. The Dragon, when exploded over a target, would encase a fifty-mile radius with flame. It would only last for ten seconds but its intense heat would disintegrate anything in its path. If the reports were accurate and the Davi was in the area, the war could be over.

****

The entry hall to ZEUS' chamber always echoed of his footsteps. Sergeant Rodger Brooks was going to meet up with Powell at the entrance after his long delay in the bathroom. Last night's dinner didn't sit well with him and he had been up all night. He usually would just let it pass but he ended up taking dye control for the problem. He didn't bother eating breakfast for his stomach still bothered him and the persistent taste of peppermint dye control was still in his throat. Powell, on the other hand, ate like a pig as usual and after watching him eat his sixth piece of greasy bacon, he excused himself from the table and told him that he would catch up with him later at the entrance. He was walking faster than usual because he was anxious to learn more about the war and the upcoming attack. Zeus would be able to give live audio and video surveillance of anything and anyone. This was going to be an exciting day, if only his stomach was into it.

He turned the corner to see Jason Powell leaning up against the steel door entrance tossing a blue illumination chip in the air. Before the two men left the chamber last night, one of the lighting fixtures blew and needed a new chip. Jason brought a replacement this morning to fix it.

"If you drop that, I'm not walking all the way back to supply to get a new one."

"No problem," exclaimed Jason as he tossed the chip in the air and then calmly caught it behind his back. "It's not like you're going to have to leave to go to the bathroom anyway."

"I don't know if it was that chicken last night or that deer meat jerky I had later, but boy did I gas up!" Rodger put his hand over his stomach and belched. The peppermint was strong. "At least the chamber has a bathroom."

"Oh, no you don't. If you have to go, you can go to the main one. I'm not going to be stuck in that stench all day." Jason turned to the palm reader on the wall next to the door and placed his right palm on the glass. "And I don't care if ZEUS could refresh the compartment; I'm not using it after you."

"Fine, I'll spare you the problem, but don't get mad at me I still remember a time when you forgot your deodorant." Rodger glanced at the palm analyzer and saw that it was still red, "Well, open the door already!"

Jason's right eye brow rose quizzically at the scanner and saw the same red light, which meant a denied access. He removed his palm, which turned the glass back to white, and then placed his palm on it again. It glowed with the bright red once again. "What the hell?"

Rodger stepped forward to the analyzer. "Get out of the way and let me try." As Jason stepped back, Rodger placed his right palm on the glass and it turned green. After a couple of high-pitched tones, the door opened quickly. "Maybe you need to rescan your palm."

"Maybe," replied Jason.

"Or maybe you have been denied access and I'm supposed to shoot you."

"Maybe I'll shoot you to put you out of your misery." Jason added as he looked at his right palm. "Oh, there's the problem, I forgot about that paper cut I got yesterday."

"That would explain it." Rodger concluded.

They walked into the room together and were instantly hit with fresh cool air. Because of all the machinery in the room, the temperature controls were set to a low setting to counteract the out-pouring heat. The room, as usual, always looked the same.

To the right was a small kitchenette that had a refrigerator, a coffee maker, sink, and storage cabinets. The cabinets contained at least two months of food supplies. A small island on the right had two bar stools attached to it and served as a small eating table. The kitchenette had everything it needed in case someone had to stay for a long period of time. It was like a small resort away from the main kitchen which proved useful when long security sweeps needed to be reviewed.

To the left of the room was the bathroom entrance which contained a shower as well as a small laundry facility. In the far back of the left side sat two sofas and a recliner. It was the place where Rodger had to always 'rest his brain'. The sofa contained a sleeper and next to it was a full closet containing extra clothes for Rodger, Jason, and Brent. A small bookshelf held several books and trinkets to give the area a lived-in look.

On the center back wall was the main console. Fourteen screens filled the wall with ever changing information. The first five screens were set primarily to all United Nations operations. The next seven screens were set to other strong countries. The last two were personal settings for Rodger and Jason. Rodger always was watching the sport reports, and Jason favored the entertainment news. Sitting below the screens was a long desk that contained two identical desks. Each side had a computer console, a chair, a file cabinet, and personal data pads. The only difference was the personal touch each side had. Pictures, cups, notes and even a plant were scattered about. The objects upon the tables were in total blackness due to the illumination chip that burned out the night before. The only thing that was lit was a large glowing green glass sphere. It was the eyes and ears of ZEUS.

"Good morning ZEUS, any new changes since our departure?" Rodger asked as he picked up the plant off his desk on the right and carried it over to the sink in the kitchen.

"Lots of activity has been started," said the electronic male voice, "all military crafts have been ordered out of the target zone,"

Jason slid on his back under the desk console and flipped open a panel. "All military? Are they that close to dropping the Dragon?"

"They have already assigned an OAJ to deliver it. Its flight time is in two hours."

A loud snap from the under-desk panel brightened the room as the desk illumination lights came on. "There, that's better." Jason said as he slid out, got up, and sat into his chair.
Rodger finished watering his plant and returned it to his desk, and then he sat down in his chair. "Can you get a vid on the air base it's flying out of?"

"Of course, I can, do you need to ask?" The voice said as the first screen flipped to a video of an Air jet base. "I can even give you the specs on the pilot, do you want to see?"

"Not interested, but I am interested on what happened in last night's game. Bring that up for me." The last screen in front of Rodger's desk flipped to the standing stats of that game.

Jason belched loudly as he reached for his data pad.

"Do I detect bacon in your breath?" questioned Zeus.

"Why yes you do," Jason replied, "and lots of it!" He stood up and walked toward the kitchen. "I'm going to make a pot of coffee."

"Please, ZEUS, don't talk about bacon," squirmed Rodger in his seat.

"Is there a problem?" Zeus inquired.

"Why yes," Jason said from across the room, "It seems that Rodger has the runs today, so DON" T let him use the bathroom in here!" He finished setting up the coffee maker and returned to his seat. "Now, if you please, bring up the entertainment news for me and start this wonderful day."

"No problem," ZEUS replied.

****

The area around the mountains was very still. The Davi knew that the opposing forces were planning an attack but were unsure of its timing. Intelligence placed the attacking forces to the west and north, cornering them in the mountains. They had been pulled back into the caves for weeks now and were getting ready to launch an aggressive sweep toward the east, a direction that no one would expect. The Davi's main attack vessels were called "Separators". The Separator was a large armed barge that could separate into three smaller vessels. Each Separator had three pilots and was armed with chemical weapons.

Their first wave was to send out three Separators to survey the area to the east and report back their findings. Once the area was clear, they were going to evacuate the area and leave behind a Terror Trap that would destroy the entire mountain and what was around it. They planned to wipe out the attacking forces with one blow.

It was time to start the Trap. Three Davi Separators slowly hovered over the mountain's east area in a distance of five miles between them. Their silent engines barely broke the stillness of the morning.

****

"There is no way Picksney could have pitched a no hitter!" Jason yelled in anger. "He's a rookie and a lousy side winding lefty!" He threw down his pen onto the table and it hit his empty coffee cup, knocking it over.

"Easy there, buddy boy", Rodger said calmly, "you lost; I won, again, naturally. Hell, if this keeps up, I could be a millionaire by the time I go home."

"There may be a problem with going home," ZEUS said breaking in, "we have a situation." A large humming started to vibrate the floor under the room. "I need you both to strap in for emergency take off."

"Emergency WHAT?" yelled Rodger. "What the hell do you mean by that?"

"Yeah," stated Jason, "and what's the problem with going home?"

"Gentleman, if you please, look at screen three and I will explain"

****

Captain Steve Morris was in the cockpit of his OAJ and was ten minutes away from the target. His head swelled knowing that he alone was going to deliver the 'Dragon' and end this war. Forces were all pulled back and awaiting the delivery. Steve knew that once the Dragon was in flight, he would have to exit the atmosphere into space to get clear of the blast. He was nervous and excited at the same time. If this war could end, he could return to his wife and child in Indiana.

****

Half a mile underground, a large humming turned into an ignition. The two pale faced sergeants were speechless after the information that ZEUS provided. He explained that the entire control center was encased in an escape ship and if he felt threatened, he could activate the ship and devastate the compound on departure. On the screens was a map of the area above them, displaying target zone, ships and the ozone factories. Zeus' conclusion was flawless. An end result that nobody could imagine.

Lieutenant Colonel Brent heard the ignition from his office and jumped out of his chair and ran for the door. He never made it to the hallway.

The escape ship shot through tons of solid rock pushing its way to the surface. After several violent shakes and tremors, the ship broke ground and demolished the barn as it exited.   Faster it rose into the air but not unnoticed. One of the Davi Separators saw it take flight and followed it in pursuit. Farther they both went out of Earth's orbit and into the atmosphere; the Separator keeping pace with the escape ship, but loosing distance from it. They quickly reached the coldness of space.

****

Several miles beneath them, Steve delivered the bomb and he, too, shot toward the atmosphere. The Dragon hit and instantaneously did its job. Steve watched how his large bomb looked so tiny from space but then started to expand. Further and further, it expanded until it was long out of the target zone. Each explosion grew bigger and brighter than the last one taking it farther from the target.

Then suddenly, unexpectedly, Earth Exploded. The blast was so intense; that it blinded Steve and he was hurtled into space from the shockwave.

Zeus was right. Each Ozone factory ignited causing a chain reaction across the planet. Temperatures in the core could not withstand the intense mix of heat and fusion that combined to an unstable element. Escape was the only solution.

Deep in space, three ships flew on paths to unknown futures ahead.

CHAPTER 2

The planet Largo was the fifth celestial body in a solar system of seven. It was the most fertile planet of them all, which is why most of the inhabitants were farmers. Largo supplied most of the food for the system, which consisted mostly of fruits and vegetables. Since the first two planets in the system, Mego and Rage, held no life, Largo had developed a large shipping company to deliver to the other four planets. The Berkley was the hottest selling crop they produced. A versatile flavorless plant that absorbed the flavor of anything it was added to. Most of the plants required cool temperatures to flourish, and Largo being on the average temperature of fifty degrees year-round it was perfect.

The cargo shipping company, Preedom, had a very technical system to ensure that the crops processing, loading, and distribution was flawless. Preedom had four bases on the planet; Kelly, Cosal, Stuart, and Serin, which all had cities built around them. The largest port, Serin Base, contained sixty-four docking hangers, thirty air pads, three main control towers and many assorted personnel. One main control tower directed all traffic around the base. Many pilots and Preedom employees distributed information to the tower and staff. A computerized system contained all ingoing and outgoing flights, the pilot's registrations, the crew members' schedules and an up-to-date report of incoming crops. Ships were always flying around the base around the clock which made Serin a very noisy place.

Serin was also the best place on the planet for entertainment and relaxation. It had several very expensive hotels, assorted restaurants, bars and shops. During travels, many pilots vacationed in Serin, which offered pressurized sound proof buildings, swimming pools, weight rooms, a theater, and complimentary ship service. Since the planet dropped down to the cool forties at night, most of the buildings on the base contained a climate control system. It provided just the right place to get away from the job and the noise.

The time was late evening and the wind had considerably picked up since the second shift at Preedom was done. Most of the workers had already eaten their meals and were all out enjoying themselves. A lot of bars around the area provided many forms of entertainment to ease the stress of space travel and work. Some bars were loud and offered an endless form of excitement, but for people who were looking for a quiet place, there were those places as well.

Liquor was always in abundance and was easily processed through a liquid purity machine. Alcohol was made in strengths, one to twenty-eight, and the higher the number, the stronger the alcohol content. Individual bars add all kinds of ingredients to the drink such as spices and fruits as well as different temperatures. Each combination creates a wide range of flavors and names.

The most expensive hotel on the base was 'Pathways'. At the front checkout desk stood a tall man in his late thirties handing his keys over to the desk clerk. He was asked to sign the checkout log and grabbed the pen from the holder. His posture was very formal, as if he was royalty, and after a quick signature, he returned the pen to the holder.

His glance slowly lifted from the book to the small man's face behind the counter. The boyish face made him snicker inside but did not cause him to lose his outer nobility. He slowly let his hand rise to his left breast pocket and pulled out his money clip. Opening the clip, he started to thumb his way through the thick stack of rolets in search for a tip.

The short clerk licked his lower chapped lips delicately. Squinting through his thick glasses, he could see a ten being gently handed to him across the counter. He reached out slowly and took the rolet from the man's hand. "Thank you, sir, for staying at The Pathways, shall I call hanger service for you?"

The tall man said nothing, just shook his head no, picked up his bag, and headed for the door.

Opening the first door, he felt the heater unit blasting him in the face as he walked toward the main outer door. At times, he thought, it was almost impossible to breathe in so much heat. His problem was solved when he opened the outer door and the noise and crisp air hit him at once.

The street was busy as usual, ships flying overhead, people talking louder to hear each other, the large steam vents of a nearby factory discharging and the whistling of the wind. Just outside the hotel was a Streetvac ship picking up trash with its vacuum intake. It added to the already over whelming noise of the night.

He stopped on the walk and looked up into the sky. Couldn't see any stars due to the bright lights of the port but he knew they were there. The problem was that they were different. The patterns were changed and even the constellations didn't exist.

Rodger Brooks was in no apparent hurry to leave although he was scheduled for a meeting the next morning. He decided to get a couple of drinks before he left, so he tossed his bag over his shoulder and started walking down the right walkway. The only bar he felt comfortable in was the busiest bar in the port, a place called 'Little Chicago'. He knew that bar well, remembered building it, and the old friend who owned it. It cost a lot to build but soon it started making huge profits and established itself as the place to be. It was located by the thirteenth hanger area and always had something going on. Every three nights was a rotation of live music, comic stand up, and then a dancing theater.

As his mind raced on, he soon found himself standing outside of the bar. The bright neon green lights of 'LITTLE CHICAGO' blazed over the top of the red brick background. He took a deep breath, sighed and opened the first door. Two women ran out in front of him laughing as they passed and one of them excused herself for cutting him off. He stepped inside and paused between the doors. It's been a while; he thought to himself, he wondered if he was still there at all. Opening the second door he was surrounded by sounds of music and tap dancing. People were clapping and cheering as well.

He saw no apparent change. The room was lowly lit with the exception of the large dance floor to the far center of the room. The stage, he remembered, was the biggest task to build. It was fifty feet long and seventy feet wide. The bar itself had seating capacity for least one hundred people and it looked like the place was past that count. Two fireplaces could be seen blazing around the room, one to the left corner wall and one to the right. The bar filled the entire left wall of the establishment, except the sitting area in the back, and was just as crowded. The right side of the room consisted of tables and dart boards. Music was playing and several dancers were tap dancing to a fast song. The flickering lights on the stage cut through the smoke and dispersed throughout the room. Everything looked cloudy.

Turning to the left, he walked up to the bar where there was an open spot in the middle. He sat his bag on the floor in front of the stool and sat down. He saw that there were four people working behind the bar but only one drew his attention. The husky black man, in his early fifties, dressed in dark blue and wearing sun glasses spotted him immediately. A large grin started to slowly engulf his face and he approached Rodger.

"Want to arm wrestle for a drink?" he asked, while propping his right arm on the bar top.

Rodger smiled, "Not today, Steve, just a galaxy drink number five."

Steve turned from the bar and went to the mixing station. To Rodger he looked a lot older than he was, definitely older since they first met. Steve was the OAJ pilot they found drifting after the explosion. Steve finished mixing the drink and walked it back over. "Jason landed in this afternoon."

"He did, huh?" Rodger mumbled

"Yep", Steve stated as he dangled the drink in front of his face, "Should I take this to his table?"

"He's here?"

"In his usual spot", Steve said as he tilted his head to the left.

"Yeah, what the hell," Rodger said while grabbing his drink, "I haven't seen him in a while." He bent down and picked up his bag and started walking toward the fireplace in the back left corner. As he approached, he couldn't help feeling that odd awkwardness every time he was around Jason, and it started to rise again. It had been a long time since they were together and a lot of things had changed. The only thing they now had in common was that they were survivors.

There he sat with a pipe, smoking up the area as if there wasn't enough smoke already. He was a little bulkier in the shoulders, a definite improvement from his old wiry body, and he had a woman sitting on his lap. She had to be one of the dancers for the dress she wore was way too short for the outside climate. As he approached, the conversation between them grew.

"How about relaxing on my sofa when you get off?" Jason said while batting his eyes.

"Sounds good, just as soon as I...." Rodger's presence stopped her from continuing.

Jason glanced up at the man before him and his smile turned sour, "Ah, Ayela, could you excuse us, please."

"Yeah," she said getting off his lap, "I'm dancing in the next act anyway."

She left the table and went back toward the stage.

Rodger slid into the chair across from Jason and sat his drink on the table. "I see you've been doing some weight lifting, "he said as he nodded toward Jason.

"Huh?" grunted Jason as he looked toward the door that Ayela went into. "Oh, the arms," he said getting his meaning, "I've been hauling shipments of thermal coolant cylinders for a while now. Just finished a run this morning"

"That's what Steve tells me," Rodger added with a sneer. "When did you start smoking that thing?"

Jason pulled the pipe out of his mouth, "Not long ago, whatcha think?"

"It makes you look different," Rodger advised, "In fact it makes you look older, Jason." He still couldn't envision Jason being thirty-five but still saw him as the pesky know-it-all who followed him everywhere he went when they were younger. And now look at him. He was dressed in a sharp looking dark blue flight jacket made of expensive leather material and black pants. He had his gun hanging from a holster around his waist and still wore his high school ring. Many things started to come to his mind, including one particular topic. "How's Sheila?"

"Same as always," Jason answered taking a puff of his pipe and blowing out the smoke. "In fact, she's not as snotty as she used to be, Hawk's tamed her down quite a bit."

"Hawk? Are you still hanging out with that kid?"

"Yes, he's still with me," Jason answered softly.

Both of them became silent and sipped their drinks, as Jason's mind started to recollect the first time, he met Hawk. It was several years ago when they first happened upon Sheila, and Rodger wanted her. The argument escalated right here at the bar and jealous hearts exploded. Jason spent more time with her than Rodger did, but his stubbornness wouldn't let her go. Soon the verbal allegations turned to fists and from there things got ugly. Steve stayed out of it, he never got between them, but this time it was not the usual fight. When Rodger pulled a knife, a small kid moved in fast and knocked the blade out of his hand. Rodger tried to move toward Jason but the kid wouldn't let him by, just kept blocking his every move. The kid was fast, unnaturally fast, in fact Steve himself commented how the he swooped in like a Hawk and disarmed him. That's how the name came about and a few days later, Rodger left, never to be seen again, until now.

"So, where is this kid now?" Rodger said before taking another sip.

"On Tego. I dropped him off on the way back here." Jason replied as he put out his pipe in the ashtray. "With all the things he could do there, I probably won't see him for a while."

He then gulped down the last of his drink and pointed to Rodger's almost empty glass. "Get you another one?"

"No, no more for me, I've got to be going." Rodger stood up out of his chair. "I have a big business meeting in the morning."

"Are you still working for that processing company?" Jason asked.

"Nope, I've got my own company now, a cargo business." He added as bent over and picked up his bag.

Steve passed by the table on his way to the bar, and Jason yelled at him. "Hey Steve, get me another seven blaster." Steve waved his hand in acknowledgment and kept walking. "Are you sure you don't want another one, Rodge?"

"No, I have to go."

"Well, in case you need any pilots, I'm available. Maybe I could run shipments for you once in a while?" Jason said with a grin.

Rodger lifted his bag over his shoulder and gave Jason an angry stare. He bent over the table placing both hands on its top. "I think it would be best to keep ourselves distant from each other," he stated in a low forceful voice, "You got what you wanted and I, well, got even better things."

The change in tone startled Jason for a moment, but he regained his control.

"Fine," Jason calmly said suddenly remembering Rodger's 'Holier-than-thou' attitude. "You've always had a temper that I didn't like anyway. I can't possibly imagine how you would be as a boss!" As Jason continued, Steve slowly walked up behind the table with Jason's drink, wary of the situation. "You even stooped as low as to try to kill me for Sheila. Well for your information she doesn't want to have a thing to do with you." Jason sighed, "I'd have to agree with her."

Rodger's anger in his eyes flared, "Now that you're finished with your usual smart assed comments, I'm going to leave before this gets out of hand."

"Only in your dreams, buddy boy, only in your dreams," Jason said while staring him down.

Rodger turned to Steve, nodded a farewell and left the bar.

Steve blew out a breath of relief, "Here you go, tough guy," he said sitting the drink on the table. He glanced back toward the door as Rodger stepped out, "Wow, for a minute there I thought you two were going to start again. Sorry I sent him over here."

"Aw, hell," Jason sighed while grabbing his drink, "forget it. He's gone and hopefully for good." Then he proceeded to drink the entire glass in one gulp.

"By the way," Steve added as he pointed to the glass, "how many of those have you had?"

"Six," Jason said as he took another drink, "Why?"

"Remember the last time when you drank too much and Sheila locked you out? It took us hours to get her to open that door!"

"Yeah, but she knows who the boss is now," he said with a grin.

"Right, like I know that's the truth", Steve said sarcastically, "and stop messing around with the dancers", he added while smacking Jason in the shoulder with the back of his hand, "By the time they get up on stage they can't concentrate on their routine."

"All the better when I get them home," Jason smiled.

CHAPTER 3

Tego was the fourth planet in the solar system and sister planet to Largo. It was a greenish blue planet, mostly rock, and produced one major product, money. Anyone lucky enough to own land on Tego would make millions. It was a place to win it all or lose everything you had. Many gambling stations littered the planet and offered ship racing, chance tables, athletic challenges and techno games. Special Arenas were widespread across the planet that offered a large assortment of challenges which included sharp shooting ranges, laser battlescopes, boxing, trick castles, death chambers and stress boxes just to name a few.

There was no officiating power in charge, not even a police security. Each owner ran their property as they saw fit. As a traveler, a person was on your own and everyone was armed with some sort of weapon. No laws governed the planet, just the individual laws of each establishment. At times it was like an ongoing party, and at other times, the most dangerous place in the system to be. The place was not for the soft of heart or the shy defenseless type. Prostitution was widely distributed and easily found. Tego, essentially, was the place to always be but never alone.

One of the largest profitable games was a Trill pit. As a gambling ring, not only did it bring in the most money but also the most casualties. The main area was a pit, thirty feet round and ten feet deep. People paid a fee to enter into the challenge. To win the challenge was a large sum of money, but it was the people who bet on the challengers that won as well. If the challenger won, they would get ten times the amount, if they lost, half the money would go to the house and the other half to the betters. Of course, there was a lot of side betting as well.

The challenger entered the pit from a door in the lower levels. They were given a short amount of time to complete the challenge and if the bells rang, it was over, and they lost. Winning was the real challenge, for once their door was shut behind them and locked, they released the Trill.

The Trill got its name by the sound it omits. An unbearable screeching within its throat, when provoked, at times could pierce the ear drums. A cornered Trill was even noisier. It had two very muscular legs that supported its thirteen-inch body, and it had no arms. Its fastest speed was forty-five specks per hour in an open field, but in an enclosed area, it was hard to control. Its large head had two pointed ears and a long nose that had several whiskers protruding out of it. Two large fangs hung out over the bottom mouth and were very poisonous. What made the Trill so odd looking were its eyes. Two large eyes, one on the left and one on the right, were bubbled out of its sockets. It could see all around its self without turning its head. A Trill came in only three colors; grey, green, and brown. The body was balanced by a seven-inch tail which was used as a weapon. It also exuded an oily residue to coat its fur which made catching a Trill a very had task indeed, which leads to the challenge.

The Challenge was won if you caught the trill, without being bitten, within the given time. Not only did the challenger win the money, but they get to keep Trill as well. Once a Trill was caught it becomes very tame to its catcher. Trills are known to be one of the best pets to have, but just the opposite can be said about the loser. A Trill's bite would knock its aggressor unconscious for several rotations and give them massive headaches for many more. If several bites occur, it could lead to paralysis. A very aggressive Trill could even tear your face off.

Deep in the District of Kota was a hole in the wall place called 'Corbin's Challenge'. It was a Trill arena that had one of the biggest payoffs and very few winners. The Trills were said to be pumped up on an adrenaline drug, although no one was able to prove it. The challengers only got three taps to catch the Trill. Individual bets were placed in the arena for either the time it took to catch the Trill, or the time it took to get bitten. The winner had to guess the exact time of the action to get a win. The noise off the crowd could be heard outside the walls of the building. Whistles, shouting and pounding was a signification sound that a challenge had just ended.

In the main office the noise became increasingly loud as two people with a stretcher came in from the pit entrance carrying a body. They passed by the front desk and could see three people standing in line, a large fairly drunk man, a tall bearded man and a boy in his later teens. They all turned their heads and watched them pass by. As the door to the pit shut, the crowd noise was muffled and the conversation in the office was easier to hear.

"I'm telling' ya, you're not going in while drunk. I don't want my Trills hurt or wounded," stated the man behind the counter. "And I don't care how much money you give me. Now take your drunken ass back upstairs and enjoy the shows before I have you escorted out." His words were backed up as one of his bouncers walked up and stood behind him at the table.

"Fine," mumbled the drunk, "I don't worry can't do"

Everyone else got a confused look on their faces as the drunk stumbled to the exit door and opened the door to the loud arena. When the door shut and the room was quite again, the owner proceeded to the next person.

"Two thousand rolets to enter and I need you to fill out a form indicating where you want us to deliver your body. If you don't have a place, the Cander Inn next door will be your drop-off spot, for an extra fee."

The Cander Inn was the worst Inns in the area. A large prostitution ring was run out of it and if you ended up there unconscious, you'd wind up probably stripped of everything you own, including your clothes. The Cander was owned by the proprietor of 'Corbin's challenge' and wasn't cheap either. It was always best to make arrangements elsewhere and of course, bring friends, always.

The bearded man threw his rolets down on the table, "Why do you assume that I'll need to be carried out?"

The owner and his guard started chuckling. "Everyone gets carried out."

The guard next to him started to laugh as the owner quickly picking up the rolets off the table, and slid a clipform at the man on the table. "Fill out your information, and we can get started."

The man picked up the pen, filled out the sheet, and spun it back toward him.

The owner looked at the sheet, tore it off the clip, and handed it back to the guard behind him. "Now, Elkin," he said with a grin, "go stand at the entrance to the pit over there, and when the light above the door goes green, enter. And nice doing business with ya."

Elken took off his jacket and hung it on a hook next to the door. "If I lose, I have friends that will be down to get me."

"They'll be called in," the man grunted.

Elkin stood there taking deep breaths, trying to concentrate on the task while staring at the red light. Suddenly, the glow changed to green, and he grabbed the door and opened it. The roar of the crowd cheering was almost deafening as he entered the arena. When the door slammed shut, silence returned and all that remained in the room was the three bouncers, the owner and the boy.

The owner glanced at the young man in front of him and snickered. He looked like he wasn't even in his twenties. He was dressed in an expensive outfit that comprised of black pants, a red shirt and a leather jacket. He slid the clipform toward him and held out his hand for the rolets. "You heard everything I said to him, boy, so fill out the form and hand over the fee."

"What's the payoff at right now?" questioned the lad as he filled out the form.

"Seven hundred forty-six thousand, eight hundred fourteen rolets, but that doesn't matter to you, boy, because you'll be out in under a tap." The owner still had his hand out for payment.

The boy finished the sheet, tore it off the clip himself and handed it to the guard. The guard yanked the sheet from him and looked at the form, "you didn't fill out your destination for your body," he noted.

"Don't need one," the boy answered, "just need the payoff when I'm done."

"Then that will be an extra three hundred rolets for your stay next door," the owner added.

"Won't need it," he replied.

Suddenly, a loud cheering emitted from the pit and two men came walking in from the arena carrying Elkin on the stretcher. Two puncture wounds, bleeding, were on his forearm. The owners' grin followed them as they left out the other door.

"How much is the payoff now?" questioned the young man.

"Listen, boy, you pay the fees for the Inn and the challenge or you don't go in, get it?" The owner quickly turned to his guard and yanked the sheet from his hand. He glanced at the boy's information and read the name. "Hawk? What kind of stupid name is Hawk?"

"That doesn't matter to you," he replied throwing all the fees on the table, "Just have my payoff ready for me when I'm done."

"Get over to the door, boy, or I'll just have one of my men throw you into the pit from upstairs." At that moment, another bouncer walked up behind the owner bent over and whispered something in his ear. The owner got a quizzical look on his face, looking the boy over, and then pointed at the pit door.

"Wait for the green, boy."

Hawk stepped up to the door and let out a sigh of impatience. He wanted to get this over and go back to the Lybec district. Lots to do, he just needed the extra rolets. Then after a couple of ticks, the light turns green, and he stepped into the arena.

The crowd was loud. He could see that he was inside a brightly lit round pit and ten feet above him was the crowd all gathered around the edge. Hands were flying around, alcohol was being passed, and smoke was rising from the assortment of men and women smoking. Once they saw who was standing in the arena, laughter started to grow louder than the cheering. The crowd's eyes followed the boy into the center of the pit and in bright neon lights; cutting through the smoke above the pit was the payoff number. It was six thousand rolets bigger than the last time. More laughter engulfed him.

Ah yes, go ahead and laugh, Hawk thought. Let's see how much you laugh when I catch the little bastard. They'll be so pissed off that charged Freon wouldn't be able to cool them down. His concentration was broken when a loud horn blared and the small door on the opposite side of the pit slid open.

The Trill ran straight out for him. It was bright green and had a very nasty growl. It was larger than most Trills, which meant they probably sent out their champion to take him out. It dead stopped right in front of him and chattered its high-pitched scream. After it looked its opponent over, it took off running to the right but before it could reach the far wall, Hawk blocked it off. The Trill then tried to run to the right but once again was blocked by Hawk. Every move it tried to make it resulted in the same conclusion. Soon the animal found itself trapped in the middle of the pit.

The crowd grew silent as they saw the speed of the boy. They started to get rowdy and throw things into the arena. Paper, boxes, bottles, food and several other items landed on the floor and started to confuse the Trill even more. The Trill circled trying to find a way past him and avoid the objects thrown into the arena at the same time. Its agitation made it screech louder with every step it took. The Trill tried to bite Hawk several times but only found air.

Suddenly, the Trill paused and cocked its head in puzzlement. It let out a questioning grunt. It had never encountered someone so fast, and it was running out of ideas. After contemplating the next move, it charged straight toward him, mouth open and screaming. Hawk jumped up and over the animal, reached down with his hand at the same time, and grabbed the back of the animal's neck. It struggled, screeched, kicked, and snapped its tail, but in a matter of ticks, it calmed down in his arms. Soon the Trill was purring in Hawk's hands.

Hawk walked to the pit entrance with his new pet and opened the door. The crowd, for the first time tonight, was quiet and stunned. Stepping into the office he walked up to the desk and was confronted with the owner, three guards and plenty of weapons. Hawk stopped in his tracks.

"So, is this him Telka?" the owner said to one of his guards.

"Oh yeah, it's him," answered the far-left man. "He's a genetically grown piece of meat, a freak of nature and a lab rat that should have died under the scope."

"So, you know him well, obviously," the owner added.

"Oh yeah, I used to work for his, ah, creator."

Hawk's eyes started to burn. "Where's my payoff?"

"There is no payoff for you, boy," the owner said yelling, "You cheated, so get out of my arena."

Hawk started to take everything in the room into sight. The three guards and the owner in front of him, the large smoky observation window behind the desk that overlooked the pit, the file cabinets to the right and the small room to the left. In that room was a table which had stacks and stacks of rolets on it.

"Watch him, guys," said Telka waving his gun, "He's fast and unpredictable."

Acting quickly, Hawk pinched the Trill. It screamed and startled the others for a brief moment and then it was thrown into the face of the owner. As it kicked, screamed and knocked the owner down, Hawk grabbed the chair to his right and threw it at Telka. As Telka fell to the floor, Hawk rushed himself to the right and hit the center guard and then the last guard before he knew what hit him. Each guard was punched three times; although it was so fast it felt like just one strong punch. They both fell unconscious to the floor as Telka jumped back up and charged Hawk, who ducked, and grabbed his charger by the arm twisting him around to face him. Telka looked into Hawk's eyes and saw them start to change. He could hear a sizzling sound as the boy's eyes turned from bright blue to completely red.

"Do you want to do this the hard way?" Hawk asked.

Telka spit blood into his face. Hawk then twisted Telka's body around and threw him at the observation window. The man's momentum carried him forward and he crashed through the glass and fell toward the pit.

A large shattering got the crowd's attention as they watched a man fall with a million of sparkling pieces of glass down to the bottom of the pit. The crash reechoed within the room and quickly the arena started to empty. Watching the people from the window frame, Hawk looked down and saw the man at the bottom. Glass and trash littered the floor and Telka remained motionless in the middle of it. A low whimper got his attention behind him and he walked back toward the desk.

There, lying on the floor, unconscious, was the owner. Several scratches were bleeding all over his face and two puncture wounds could be seen on his neck. Sitting next to him, was the Trill, who quizzically looked up at him and whined.

"Come on, my friend," Hawk said reaching down with his arm. The Trill scampered up it and sat upon his right shoulder. Hawk then reached over and grabbed a satchel that he saw earlier and looked down at the owner.

"And thanks for the bag, boy," he said smiling at the unconscious man. He then walked to the back room to fill the bag with rolets.

CHAPTER 4

The front room was carpeted in dark brown shag and suited the plush maroon furniture quite well. The fully equipped kitchen was open on the right and held enough space for a family of five for a week. To the left of the room were doors that led to the bedroom containing a king size firmmat, two end tables, a video entertainment screen and a large walk-in closet. At the far end of the bedroom was another door which led to the bathroom containing a marbled stand-alone tub.

Jason walked out of the bathroom carrying the rest of his belongings with him. He approached the bed and put the toiletries into a travel bag sitting upon it. He was all ready to leave with the exception of a few items which still remained in the wall safe. He walked over to the right side of the bed where a programming pad was on the wall and typed in numbers into the keypad, and a panel opened up in the wall. Inside were his seven-sixteen laser pistols, the holster and a couple of other personal items.

He pulled out the holster belt and strapped it around his waist. He always had it hanging low to his right side, about arm's length, so that he could get at his gun in a hurry. Next, he reached in for the pistol, feeling the cold metal sent a shiver down his arm. He had fallen in love with it ever since he acquired it on Tego several years ago. He was anxious to use it again, to hear its blast, to see it burst and to feel its power. Unfortunately, the only shooting arenas were on Tego. Just looking at its shiny stock brought back memories. The San Crestley run, the spiked caves of Faitio and the mystery castle of Badron was just a few visions that danced in his mind. He slid the pistol into the holster and tapped it.

Next, he reached in for his watch, which stunned him that it was still running. He shook his head in amusement and saw that the time was six thirty-five, Central Standard Time. Of course, this system had a totally different way of timing things and, different words to describe them. Seconds were ticks, minutes were taps, hours were courses and days were rotations. Also, according to the analog, it would have been Friday the thirteenth. He smiled thinking about its old meaning. The watch wasn't kept for just the memories but also, Steve, Rodger, and he used it for their own personal timekeeping.

The thought of Rodger infuriated him again, and he shook his head to shake it off.

Reaching into the safe again he grabbed the remaining object, a necklace chain containing his military dog tags. He wore them to always remind himself about what the ultimate sacrifice was to be, dying for a cause greater than life itself. He slipped the necklace over his head and zipped up his jacket.

Tossing his bag over his shoulder, he gave the room one last glance. It was a very comfortable room and expensive as well, but it suited his taste. He was there for four days and just got bored really quick. It was a great get away place, but it was now time to move on. He slowly stepped from the bedroom and to the front door, glancing around to catch if he missed anything. When he reached the door, he pushed the pad, and the door slid open.

As he walked down the hall, and as Jason exited, he considered his options. He could check to see if Preedom was looking for any pilots, check any clubs for anyone who needed special runs or just go join Hawk on Tego. When he reached the open elevator door, he stepped inside and rode it down to the lobby floor.

The music playing in the elevator made him smile. No matter where you travel, whether it be another planet or another solar system; the music in elevators always sucked.

When the elevator opened, he could see the glamour of the lobby. A large chandelier hung in the center of the room and dazzled the walls with its sparkling glass. He estimated its weight to be about five to six hundred pounds and underneath it was the main waiting area. Several people were sitting on sofas with their luggage next to them under the chandelier. Jason stepped out of the elevator and walked the long way around to the front desk on the other side. He just didn't trust anything to hold that much weight. When he got to the other end of the room, he walked up to the desk to check out where a young lady behind the counter smiled as he approached with his key card.

"Can I help you sir?" she questioned with a smile.

"Yes, I need to check out of room forty-one." He said as he laid the card on the counter.

"Not much of a vacation," she said as she looked up his account on screen, "you just checked in four rotations ago. Was everything alright?"

"Everything was fine, just got bored."

"Did you look at the entertainment program that we offer?" she said while pointing toward the left.
"Actually, I'm not here for a vacation, just wanted to get away for a while from the regular routine." Jason said while pulling out his pipe, "Do you have a light?"

"A what, sir?" she quizzically said.

"I'm sorry, I mean a blaze."

"Yes sir." She said as she reached into a drawer in her desk. She laid two packages on the counter. "Can I get you anything else?"

"No, thank you, just my final bill, please."

She turned the screen toward him and saw it was two hundred and thirty-five rolets. He pulled three hundred out of his pocket and handed it to her. "Keep the change."

"Sir!" she said loudly, "I can't take this big of a tip!"

"Don't worry about it," he said holding up his hand, "if it's too much, split it with someone, perhaps the bell hop or the cleaning staff. Just don't give it to the hotel."

She smiled again, "Thank you, sir, have yourself a good night and please come again."

Moving away from the counter, he opened the box and lit his pipe with a blaze. The tobacco gleamed bright red as he sucked it into his lungs. Once it was lit, he threw the expired blaze into the can next to the entrance door and then stepped outside. The heating unit between the doors blew his pipe smoke all around his head making a cloud around him. When he stepped out the second set of doors, the smoke totally blew dissipated.

He stood just outside the entrance, the large lit sign of the Grand Gate Hotel casting a green glow on the walk way in front of him. The chill in the air with the breeze had the temperature around thirty-eight degrees, and he could see his breath as much as the smoke from his pipe. He contemplated on going to Steve's but didn't want to walk that far in the cold, so he decided to take the alternative route.

Underground there were several tunnels that ran between sections in the port. They were not heated but at least they were out of the wind. It was how they used to get around before the upper port was built, before the techno advancement. Not many people visiting Serin base knew they were there, only the locals. Just a block away was an entrance that would come up close to Steve's but it was twice the distance.

A sudden gust of wind hit him and his pipe almost flew out of his mouth. 'That was it', he thought. 'Tunnel, here I come.'

He started walking toward the right, where the entrance was, and stuffed his hands into his pockets. It amazed him to no end that this cold climate was good for the crops. Back on Earth, everything would have died, and farmers would have no jobs.

Reaching an iron door to the right of the walkway, Jason opened the door and walked down the flight of steps in front of him. After three steps, the door slammed shut and echoed in the area. It was cool and quiet but no breeze was present. When he reached the bottom of the steps, he turned to the left and started walking down the long-curved hall. Several light flares were out which made him wonder who replaced them when it was needed. The tunnel itself had several connecting tunnels which made it easy for anyone to get very lost. He took several puffs from his pipe and the cherry taste stung his tongue lightly, making him lick his lips. With every turn he took, the smoke from his pipe left a trail behind him.

Once again, his mind drifted toward Rodger. He couldn't understand how someone that you knew for such a long time could turn on you and hate you so much. They tried running an arena on Tego and since then Rodger had changed. Money and greed took him over and he was never the same.

When he turned left around another corner, a familiar sound came to his inner ear, a sound that he knew very well.

Hum* "I heard you ran into Rodger at Steve's," the female voice said inside him.

"That was last night," Jason said out loud, "get yourself ready, after I have a few drinks with Steve we're leaving this rock."

Hum* "I am ready, and what's this about you straightening me out?" the voice said angrily.

"All right, Sheila, don't start that crap again," he answered harshly, "I'm really not in the mood to argue."

Hum* "How many drinks are you planning to have?"

"As many as I want." He turned the corner and noticed all the lights were out down the next hall, "Damn it!"

Hum* "What?"

"All the lights are out; I'm going to have to feel my way down this one." Jason sighed.

Hum* "Why the hell are you in the tunnels?"

"To keep my butt from freezing off," he answered as he put his right hand along the wall to guide himself along.

Hum* "If you would have taken the heavier jacket like I told you..."

"Oh, shut up, will ya?"

Hum* "Well you started it with your, 'I'll be just fine strut,' when you left."

"If you don't stop your nagging, I'm...."

Hum* "JASON, DON'T YOU DARE SHUT ME OFF!"

"Daring me?" he said as he smiled in the darkness, "You know I'll do it."

Hum* "So, how was your get away at the Grand Gate?"

"Fine, and don't try to change the subject. Just get ready and I'll be there in a couple of hours."

Hum* "I AM READY!"

Jason shook his head as his blind pace continued down the hall. The hall became so dark that he ended up placing both hands along the wall to guide himself. After several steps he started to realize that his choice on directions was proving to be wrong. His hands slid along the cold stone walls until he touched onto something different, something soft, plump like a women's....

"Oh! Excuse me!" he said pulling his hands back, "I didn't see you there."

The drunk girl answered, "That's ok, mister, I saw your flare as you walked down the hall. Got any time tonight?"

Recognizing the voice, Jason answered. "Jetta, what the hell are you doing?"

"Jason," she yelled as she wrapped her arms around him, "What ya doing, where ya going, can I come?"

"I'm getting ready to go off planet, "he answered as he tapped out his now dead pipe and proceeded to put it in his inside pocket.

"Take me! Take me! I'll keep you warm on those cold nights!" she said as she hugged him tighter.

Jason grabbed her arm and pulled her off, "Sorry, but no. I don't know when I plan to return. It could be a while and I know how much you would miss this place."

"You mean I'll never see you again?"

"No...maybe...I don't know. But if I return, I know where to find you."

"I know you do, "she said while puckering for a kiss. Of course, Jason couldn't see it and continued down the hall.

"Say hello to Salvo for me." He yelled from further down the walkway, but no answer was returned. She had either passed out or just completely phased out.

Hum* "Who was that?"

"You know who it is."

Hum* "Yeah, that door-to-door whore, why didn't you grab something?"

Jason's expression turned to puzzlement, "What do you take me for, a sexual predator?"

Hum* "Not bad, but you said it, I didn't"

Upon the next turn, Jason saw a little light at the end of the hall and toward the left, and he was able to pick up his pace. The coast was clear of any objects, or people. When he got to the end where the light was at, he had to squint due to the large brightness of the flame. He could see all the way down toward the end of the next tunnel and he knew that it ended in a large open area. The area was his exit. Soon he would be sitting down in his favorite chair, next to a raging fire place and drinking a galaxy seven. Or maybe a drinking a firehouse eight, or …….

A scream down the hall ended his thoughts.

Hum* "What was that?"

"I don't know, sounded like a woman screaming." He said slowing his pace.

Hum* "it's probably that slut again, she…"

"No," Jason said cutting her off, "This is in the opposite direction. Sounds like someone's in trouble," he said while slowly laying his bag on the floor, "Keep quiet; I'm going to check it out." He started walking toward the noise.

Just inside the exit door, a woman laid on her right-side unconscious on the floor. Her long blond hair covered her face. Two men stood over the top of her; both dressed in ragged torn clothing, unshaved, and with a loss of personal hygiene.

"Why did you hit her so hard?" asked the smaller of the two as he knelt down and started going through her purse.

"I just didn't want to deal with all that kicking and screaming," the lower voice said.

The smaller man stuck a small light bar in his mouth and dumped the contents of her purse on the floor. "Hey," he exclaimed, "lookie what we have here!" He held up an orange security tag, "we got ourselves a higher authority!"

"And," the other man added, "A rich one!" he said picking up a large pad of rolets.

The smaller man reached over to her and flipped her on her back. "Do you think she might have anything in her pockets?"

"Maybe, But I'd bet she's got something under those clothes!" The larger one got down on his knees and ripped open her blouse exposing a delicate flowered bra. Pulling out his knife, he cut the bra in half and flipped open the sides. Her breasts glistened with beads of sweat in the light.

"Wow," the other one exclaimed, "She's got some beauties!"

Suddenly a large laser blast blew a hole into the wall right behind the larger man's head. They both jumped to their feet and looked down the darkened hall. A groan to the right of them made them turn their heads to see the woman slowly regaining consciousness. She sat up and when she saw the two men, slid backwards on her butt and up against the wall. They turned their attention away from her and looked back down the hall again.

Jason had slowly put out each flame as he passed them, hiding himself in the darkness. He had his pistol out and was ready to fire his next shot. He just wanted to ensure that the woman wasn't going to get hit in the crossfire.

"Let's get out of here," the smaller man said.

"Nothing doing," said the larger one. "Nobody is going to take a pot shot at me and get away with it." He reached down with his left hand and pulled out his gun.

Another shot fired from out of the darkness and pierced the hand holding the gun. The man screamed and dropped his weapon. The smaller man ran out the exit door as the other man tried to pick up the gun with his right hand. Another shot fired out and hit the door behind him

"GET OUT OF HERE!" yelled Jason down the hall. The large man hesitated, thought about it, and then ran out the door as well. The door slamming echoed many times in the hall.

The woman on the floor started to wake up and only heard silence. Was she dead? She couldn't and didn't want to open her eyes in fear of what was standing in front of her. She felt cold, clammy, stiff and still up against the wall. Every part of her body felt like a lead weight, a piece of concrete attached to the foundation. Movement was the last thing on her mind. She started to shiver uncontrollably, not knowing what to expect as she slowly opened her eyes and saw a man standing in front of her.

"Are you ok?" Jason asked while glancing at the battered woman. He saw that she was bleeding badly from a cut on her forehead and cautioned a possible fracture. Slowly walking up to her, he asked again, "Are you alright?"

Her lips couldn't move. Her mind was confused and scared.as she started to tremble all over and she drew her knees up toward herself. She wanted to crawl away but couldn't for she was backed into the corner. She slowly opened her mouth.

"I...I....I..." was all she could get out.

Jason knelt down to her, "They're gone, no need to be afraid anymore, I'll see to that."

His words were soothing to her ears. She could feel sweat sting her eyes as she saw him reach out with his right hand.

"Take it easy," he said calmly, "let me help you up."

She saw the outstretched arm and it sent a chill up her spine. Should she grab this stranger's arm or run? Was he going to attack her as well? Should she scream?

"I know you're confused," he added while pushing his hand forward again, "but I could have just kept on walking."

The thought of what would have happened if he did, woke her up. She grabbed his hand, pulled herself up, and gave him a strong hug.

Jason put his arms around her holding her securely. He could feel her cold body up against his and could hear her crying.

Hum* "Go for it!"

Jason said nothing but cursed within. He then lifted his right hand up behind his right ear and tapped the skin. The Hum stopped. Her grip tightened so much on him that it was getting hard to take breaths.

"Relax," he said on what little air was left, "I think you're going to crack one of my ribs."

She pulled her head back and looked into his eyes as she lessened her grip, "Sorry," she said with a very soft raspy voice.

"It's ok," he said taking in a deep breath, "you're safe now."

She nodded her head. Her mascara was running down her cheeks on her face and dripped off her chin. Slowly, she let her arms drop from his body and leaned back on the wall with a thump. Jason glanced down at her breasts as they bounced when she hit the wall and she followed his eyes. She saw her condition, blushed and then put her arms over them for cover.

Jason unzipped his blue jacket and handed it to her. She smiled and took it from him. He turned away to let her dress herself and then knelt down to her scattered contents on the floor. He started picking up the items and returned them to her purse. After he picked up the last item, he stood and turned toward her. She had his flight jacket on, zipped up and held a bra in her right hand that was in two pieces.

"Looks like they got all of your rolets," he said while nodding toward her, "and they got your bra."

She started slowly laughing and then uncontrollably started to cry.

"Come on," he said gently, "We better gets that gash on your head fixed before it gets infected."

"Gash?" she said as she lifted her left hand up to her forehead. She felt a large lump and wetness and when she pulled down her hand; her palm was covered in blood.

Jason caught her before she hit the floor.

CHAPTER 5

She slowly awoke to a soft cozy sensation. Her body was so relaxed in the warmth of the heavy blanket that she felt paralyzed. The heat soothed her muscles and her back felt so relaxed. She felt like she was wrapped up in paradise, a comfort zone that she didn't want to let go. The smell of the sheets was so fresh it made her think of gaggle flowers in a meadow. As she stretched out her arms, she felt the headboard of the bed and its carpeted inlay.

Carpeted????

She suddenly snapped to awareness as she realized that this wasn't her bed. Sitting up quickly, she started to take note of her surroundings. She was in a bedroom but where and how, she did not know. The decorations on the walls and the looks of the furniture told her that it was not a cheap place. She pulled open the covers and saw that she still had on the flight jacket that the man handed her. Her lightheadedness slowly shook from her as she recollected with what had happened. She reached up to her forehead and felt a bandage.

Noise coming from a door toward her left made her jump off the bed, making her a little dizzy from the fast move. She stumbled and grabbed the head board to catch herself. Her grogginess made her legs unsteady, but she soon regained her stance and walked to the door.

Jason heard the door to the bedroom open as he was standing in the kitchen. He turned to see her stagger into the room.

"Good morning," he said softly, "are you feeling any better?"

"I'm really dizzy," she said taking a few steps into the room.

"Rest yourself in that recliner and I'll get you something to drink." he said while pointing to the chair.

She gingerly walked over to the chair and sat down. The soft cushions almost swallowed her body as it sank her in.

Jason opened the refrigerator and grabbed a green bottle off the top shelf, "Do you like Berkley Juice?"

"Berkley juice? I haven't had that in a long time."

He opened the bottle and started filling a glass on the counter, "The vitamins and electrolytes should give you a boost," he said as he put the bottle back into the refrigerator. As he picked up the glass and started walking toward her, he noticed her glancing around the room.

"Do you like the room?" Jason asked as he noticed her curiosity. "I had no problem getting it back. I just checked out of here last night."

"Where are we?" She questioned as she took the glass from him.

"We're at the Grand Gate Inn."

Her eyes widened at the answer as she took a sip of the juice. She could feel its smoothness flow down her throat as it warmed her within.

"I patched up the cut on your head, "he stated as he sat down on the sofa next to the table between them, "it's nothing serious, might leave a scar."

"Thanks," she said.

"You're welcome, Katrina." He replied.

Her left eyebrow slightly rose in puzzlement, "How did you know my name?"

"Your ID was lying on the floor when I picked up your belongings last night."

"Oh," she said while taking a drink, and then realizing his statement, she sat up quickly.

"Last night? What's the time?"

"' No idea, but it's been daylight for some time now."

"I've got to get to work," she said setting the empty glass on the table. Her abrupt movements made her dizzy, and she held her hand up to her head. "Oooo, that wasn't a good idea," she mumbled.

"I think you have a good excuse for not going; besides your head isn't ready for the stress of the tower."

She lifted her brow again. "How much more did you read off that card?" she asked curiously.

"Just enough,"

"That's not fair, you know me but I don't know you."

"The names Jason Mathew Powell," he said standing up and grabbing her empty glass. "Would you like some more juice?"

"Please," she said. "Why such a long name?"

"I never really thought about it, "he said walking toward the kitchen and retrieving the bottle again, "just a name, that's all." He filled her glass again and walked it back to her.

"What do you do?"

"You mean line of work?" he said while sitting down again.

"Yes", she said taking another sip.

"Well," he spoke while trying to word it, "I cargo product for businesses if the price is right."

"So, you're a smuggler?"

"So I am," he admitted as she leaned back on the sofa, "Are you ok with that?"

"Oh yes, in fact I find it rather inviting. The adventures, the surprises, even the unexpected. It would never get boring!"

Jason smiled, "Hate to upset you, but it gets very boring."

"Oh, yeah," she stated, "try being a control Tower Operator. That is a sleeper job" She took another sip from her glass, "So do you travel a lot?"

"Whenever needed," he said with a sigh.

Her eyes widened at a though, "Do you have your own ship?"

"Yep."

"Wow!" she exclaimed as she slowly sat up, "Is it a freighter or a cargo barge?"

"Well.....a....I mean...it's..."

"I'm sorry, I'm asking too many personal questions," she interrupted, "I've always been intrigued with ships and none of my other friends have a ship."

"Other friends, "Jason said leaning forward, "so I take it I'm added to the list?"

Katrina smiled, "A man who saves your life, doesn't take advantage of you when you're unconscious, heals your wounds and gives you the comforts of his home is not what I call an enemy."

"Thanks," he smiled back, "it feels good to be accepted and no, you're not asking too personal questions, just complicated ones to answer." He looked toward the kitchen and back toward her, "Are you up to walking somewhere to get a bite to eat?"

"Oh yes," she said holding her stomach, "I'm surprised you haven't heard my stomach growling."

Jason pointed to the bathroom. "If you want to freshen up, there are fresh towels in the bathroom but be careful of the tub, you can lose track of time in that thing."

She stood up slowly and turned toward him. "Thanks for this," she said pulling on the bottom of the jacket, "I'll have it cleaned as soon as I get home to change."

"No rush."

She walked to the bedroom, entered, and shut the door behind her.

As she stood next to the sink, she looked up into the mirror and saw the bandage and bruise on her face. She had a purplish haze around her left cheek bone and the bandage covered her entire left fore head. Her left shoulder felt sore and probably was bruised as well. She walked over to the tub and turned on its water, feeling the temperature with her right hand. Once she had adjusted the faucets, she then turned and locked the door. Even though he saved her life, he was still a stranger and she felt safer knowing that it was locked. She unzipped the jacket, hung it on the back of the door, and proceeded to undress.

Meanwhile, Jason started making a pot of hot kedy brew. Its aroma was soothing but how he missed the taste and smell of fresh ground coffee. Kedy brew was the closest thing to coffee that he found, and it did take several months for him to get used to the taste. If only he would have had some hazelnut or butter pecan cream to go with it like Lt Brent had. His thoughts drifted back to what seemed like a previous life time and he pulled out his tags from his shirt and clutched them in his hand. Dear friends and family gone but not forgotten.

When she stepped out of the tub, she felt refreshed. All her problems seemed to rinse off her body and exit through the drain in the bottom. She didn't feel comfortable putting on the dirty clothes again, but she would head straight home and change after they ate. When she opened the door Jason was sitting on the sofa smoking his pipe. The smell of the smoke filled her lung's and she coughed a couple of times

"Sorry about the smoke," Jason said waving his hand trying to clear the air. "It's a nasty habit I acquired." He put the pipe into a tray on the table, "It beats biting my nails."

At that time, Katrina started laughing and held up her hands. His eyes caught sight of her short-ragged nails. "Maybe I should start smoking?" she laughed again. She walked back to the recliner and slowly sat down on it. She started looking around the room and took note of its rich glamour. "This isn't your permanent place; you did say that you had no trouble getting it back. Were you leaving?"

"Actually, yes,"

"Did you have another job?"

"No, just wanted to get off world." Jason sighed, "I was getting bored."

"Bored! You're obviously caught up in the tourist propaganda. I could show you a few places." She smiled.

"I'd like that," he said standing up, "Are you ready for some food?"

"Yes," she said hastily as she stood carefully up not to rush her head.

Jason presented his hand toward the door, "Then, shall we?"

They left the apartment together and soon found themselves in the lobby. All the way down she was telling him all about her job at the tower and her responsibilities. She was a very fascinating person, and he found her to be quite intelligent. She seemed shy but strong willed at the same time. They continued out the exit and started walking toward a place called 'The Station', a restaurant known for its breakfast. The food there was a high-class rating and served many varieties.

While walking on the main street, the morning sun was blinding to the eyes but the warmth was welcomed. During the walk, Katrina told Jason about different spots around the base and places you don't want to go. He knew some of the areas but several places she mentioned he had never heard of them. She was especially thrilled to talk about a lake that was to the north of the Base. She loved nature and getting away from the busy everyday traffic of the base. She loved to camp and tried to get out there at least three times a cycle.

Several taps later, they found themselves at the entrance to the restaurant and were immediately seated. Jason pulled her chair out for as she sat down. The service was prompt, quick and they soon found themselves eating a feast.

"Oh, this suscal is so delicious," she said taking a sip of her drink, "it just melts in your mouth."

"Glad you like it, it's my favorite dish in the place. In fact, I had a hard time trying something else. Once you get stuck on something you truly like, it's hard to break away."

"So true..." she stated. "I was stuck on casser juice for a long time once to the point where my tongue started to get a lovely shade of orange. I had so much during that period that now I can't even bring myself to have a glass now. I overdid it, and it just doesn't taste the same." She took another bit of her suscal and then looked down at Jason's right arm, "By the way, what is that on your right wrist?"

"A watch," Jason said while holding his hand forward for her to see. "It keeps time."

"Interesting," she said squinting at the object, "I usually just have a TDC in my pocket. I can never go anywhere without it. If I need the time, it's there; if I need the date, it's there, if I need to talk to someone, it's there. Without it I would be totally lost."

Hum* "Doesn't this Bitch ever shut up?"

"Oh, shut up." Jason said out loud.

Katrina's face froze, her mouth gapped open, and her expression turned hurtful.

Jason held his hand to his mouth, "I'm sorry, Katrina, I wasn't talking to you. I have a communication device that just turned back on."

Hum* "Actually, I've been on for an hour and a half to be exact, damn this slut can jabber, why don't we…"

"Sheila, give me a chance to explain, will ya?"

Katrina's puzzled look turned into a quizzical smirk, "You have an implanted comchip transmitter?"

"Why, yes," he answered, "It's imbedded into my inner ear. She can hear everything I do and the only way I can talk to her is to speak out loud."

"This, she," Katrina said, "is she you wife?"

"Oh no," Jason laughed, "Not a chance."

Hum* "Why, what's wrong with me?"

"Nothing is wrong with you," Jason said out loud.

"I didn't ask," Katrina stated.

"I wasn't talking to you, I was…. oh, hell with it!" he exclaimed as he turned and flagged down the waiter for the check, "How would you like to meet her?"

"If you insist," she said hesitantly while she wiped her mouth with her napkin and then placed it on her plate. "I'm ready any time."

The waiter arrived with the check, and Jason slipped a rolet to his open palm. They both got up from the table and soon found themselves outside. Jason held out his right arm and Katrina wrapped her left arm around it. They started walking toward the direction of the cargo bays.

"You mentioned that the device just turned on," Katrina stated, "how does it go off?"

Hum* "When she gets in your pants, she'll see how it goes off."

Jason rolled his eyes, "I have a button just under the skin behind my right ear. It will shut the connection off for two hours."

"Two what?" she said quizzically.

"I'm sorry, I mean two courses."

Hum* "Speaking of courses, is she the dessert?"

"Oh, you're funny," said Jason.

Katrina slowed and got a quizzical look on her face again, "It's really hard to tell if you're talking to me, or her."

"No need to worry,' Jason added, "She's just getting jealous."

Hum* "Jealous, OF THAT?"

"I don't want to start any trouble" Katrina sadly said.

Hum* "What an airhead, I bet all her brains are in her boobs. You should squeeze one and see if she gets a headache."

"Now that was downright rude!" yelled Jason as he stopped.

Katrina, once again, thought he was talking to her. "Why is that rude?"

"Not, you, her," Jason tried to explain. "She said things about you and called you a few names."

"What? I've never met this person and already she calling me names? What did she say?"

"Oh, no," he said shaking his head, "I'm not telling you."

"Please?" Katrina said softly.

Hum* "Please?"

"Alright, but don't get mad at me." He took a deep breath and let it out slow, "She called you an airhead and slut."

Hum* "Don't forget Bitch!"

Katrina's anger started to boil, "Well of all the....."

Hum* "I'm not jealous..."

"You are, too." Jason answered.

Katrina looked hurt, "So you agree with her?"

"No.....I...." Jason screamed out loud. "Oh, forget this shit, follow me, Katrina."

He turned right at the next corridor that led to the front of loading dock bays and picked up his pace. Katrina's short quick steps tried to keep up with Jason's long stride and it almost made her trip. When she finally caught up with him, he was stopped in front of hanger number thirty-seven. He pulled a bay door opener out of his pocket and pushed the button

Slowly the doors started to lift.

"Katrina," he said as the door fully opened and the lights popped on, "Meet Sheila."

There, sitting inside was a small silver travel ship.

Hum* "Hello, Bitch", said the front speaker in a snotty attitude.

CHAPTER 6

"Sheila," Katrina said, pointing at the ship, "That's her?"

Hum* "Disappointed?" sounded from her front speaker again.

"No, not at all, I think you're beautiful!"

Hum* "Oh yes, of course I am. Don't you wish you could be me, ya know, Beautiful?"

"Define beautiful," Jason said as he took his pipe out and started filling it.

Hum* "According to Franchezes Universal Dictionary; beautiful is defined as the highest degree of pleasure to the senses or the mind."

Jason turned and glanced at Katrina, "You took the words right out of my mouth."

Katrina smiled back and felt kind of coy as she tilted her head down.

Hum* "Oh boy, what a line! and by the way, DON'T SMOKE THAT DAMN THING IN HERE!"

Jason stopped putting tobacco in the pipe and he pocketed it.

Katrina shook her head, "I still can't believe that this ship is talking to me. You're not playing a joke on me, are you? Is there someone inside that thing speaking on a microphone?"

Hum* "THING? THING? This so-called thing happens to be my body, bitch, where did you get yours, out of the garbage?"

"THAT'S ENOUGH," yelled Jason, "you can stop with that kind of talk NOW! Stop being such a pain in the ass!"

Hum* "Pain in the ass? THAT was uncalled for."

"Shut up and open the door, it's freezing out here." Jason said as he started walking toward her right side.

Hum* "Let you in? Not on your life, not after what you just said."

Jason stopped and turned toward Katrina, "I'm sorry for all of this, she really isn't this bad."

"Why are you apologizing?" Katrina questioned, "Nobody should have to apologize for someone else's actions?"

"I agree, but I was responsible for most of her programming, it's kind of embarrassing."

Hum* "At least the creative part, Hawk helps with the techno stuff."

Katrina tilted her head, "Hawk?"

"I'll tell you inside, open up Sheila." Jason repeated as he continued walking toward her right side.

Hum* "Not until you apologize."

"OK, OK, I'm sorry."

Hum* "Cross your heart?"

"OPEN THE DAMN DOOR!"

A low grinding noise produced a small ramp that slid out of her back right side and lowered to the ground. When it made contact, a loud hiss accompanied the sliding door at the top of the steps. Jason started to approach the steps but Katrina was still in awe looking at what was in front of her.

Yes, Sheila was a thing of beauty. She was completely silver and the lights in the hanger made her shine. She had a very small bridge, about twenty feet in diameter, and was a perfect sphere which contained two large black stained windows that made her look like some sort of bug. The glass was so dark that it was impossible to see inside, which is why Katrina thought there was a trick being played on her. The front speaker was just below the middle of the windows and it looked like her mouth. The most interesting part of her was her wings. They started at the top of her body and arched up out and then back down making the effect of two rainbows side by side. Each of them contained a weapon at the tip's end. Then she noticed something odd, Sheila had no landing legs. She simply just hovered about three feet off the ground.

Katrina started walking toward the door where Jason stood waiting. She couldn't help staring at this wonder in front of her and her pace slowed. She saw that every part of her body was very smooth, not a ripple or a bump on it. Looking at her from the side, she saw that the contour of her body slimmed back from her bridge and rounded off at a point bringing her to be about fifty feet long. She couldn't help but notice that....

Hum* "what's the matter, space case, are you chicken to step inside?

"No, I'm just taking you all in; you look so...so..."

Hum* "Intelligent, magnificent, radiant, brilliant, fantastic..."

Jason cut in, "......irritable, testy, moody, grouchy, tempered,"

Katrina started laughing. Then she noticed when she got closer to her body, that Sheila was covered in small clear glass circles. Each one was only an inch in diameter and covered her whole body. They ran in a straight line, around the top to the bottom and from side to side. Each circle was five feet apart from each other.

"What are those clear objects?" Katrina asked.

"Those are her sensors, pretty much how she sees," Jason answered

Katrina's eyes widened, "You mean she has perceptional ocular units?"

Jason's draw dropped.

Hum* "Well!" Sheila spoke in surprised, "You're smarter than I thought. Do you know what an open system cyclotronic evaporator is?"

"Cool it off, Sheila," Jason said taking the first step, "She's..."

"Why, yes, I do." answered Katrina.

Both Jason and Sheila were speechless, for cyclotronic were very rare, practically extinct.

Hum* "Define cyclotronic."

Katrina started to answer, "It's the...."

"Wait, Katrina," Jason said cutting her off, "I believe you know what it is; Sheila's just trying to make you look stupid. Now come on, let's get inside."

She saw Jason walk up and enter Sheila as she walked underneath the right wing. She soon found herself up the steps and inside as well.

When the door slid shut behind her, she saw that they were standing in a small hallway that ran down the middle of the ship. The warmth inside was very cozy, but the lights were very low. The hallway was about fifteen feet long and consisted of two openings, one on each side. She also noticed one of the ocular units on the ceiling in the hall. As she followed Jason down the hall, she peered into the opening on the right. Inside were two beds, an end table, a dresser and another door. Two steps more she saw that the door on the left contained a small kitchen unit and a table. Each of the rooms also contained an ocular unit on the ceiling. As she followed Jason toward the front, she didn't see the steps leading to the upper level and fell down onto her right knee.

"OUCH," she yelled as the tingling pain shot up her leg.

Jason turned quickly to help her up, "I'm sorry about that, Sheila could you turn the lights up?"

The room went pitch black.

"Sheila," Jason spoke angrily, "this isn't funny, turn them up now!"

Hum* "What you waiting for, dummy, she can't see you. The bedrooms just down the hall!"

Katrina didn't know what to think. Here she was, on the floor, in the dark, with a searing pain running in her knee. She was in so much pain to begin with from last night that her whole body felt stiff. Now her knee was going to be sore as well.

Jason blindly slamming his fist into the wall made Katrina jump. "TURN THEM UP NOW!" he yelled.

The lights slowly glowed.

"So, help me, Sheila, I'll stay at the hotel for weeks and never talk to you!"

Bright lights flashed across the interior as if the sun itself moved in. Both Jason and Katrina had to cover their eyes to adjust. Jason helped her stand and she started rubbing her knee.

"Are you ok?" Jason asked.

"I'm fine, but I can imagine the bruise I'm going to have"

They finished walking up the steps and the short walk led to the bridge. It was very comfortable looking. A circular counter ran about three feet above the floor all around the inner part of the bridge. It contained two swivel chairs and assorted drawers. Just above the counter were the two smoked glass windows. Jason motioned for her to sit down in the right chair as he sat down in the left. The cushion was so soft, it soothed her tired body.

"I wish the chairs in the tower were this comfortable," Katrina sighed, "they're like sitting on a rock."

"Well, they were really expensive, and it was Hawk who found them. He's got a pretty good talent of finding things."

"You mentioned this Hawk before, who is he?"

"A young man I met a while ago, and we hang out together."

"Like a partner?"

"Yeah, you could say that. He's been on several runs with me, and we've been in some pretty sticky situation together." Jason smiled at the thoughts.

"Where is he now?"

"On Tego"

Hum* "Jabber, jabber, jabber…" omitted the speaker on the ceiling above their heads, "Jason why don't you cut out all this yackity, yackity bullshit and get down to some serious sex?"

Katrina gasped, and Jason kicked the wall in front of him, "One more crack like that, and I'll rent another vessel for my next run!"

Hum* "Ok, I'll be polite, it's not like she's the only girl you've brought in here."

Katrina gave Jason a look and shook her head in disdain. Looking around the bridge again, she noticed something missing, "Where is the equipment to control her?"

Hum* "Nobody controls me, sister, I control myself. I need no hand holding or nose wiping!"

"She could use a diaper change, though," Jason added.

Katrina laughed, "She is different, but she looks too small to be a cargo ship."

"Well," Jason said leaning back in the chair, "She was originally an escape pod, but with a lot of modifications. "

"Escape from what?" Katrina questioned.

Jason's face became blank, "The only place I called home."

Suddenly an aroma hit the air that could only be explained as a spoiled egg fart. Jason got a really bad look on his face and Katrina winched at the smell. Both of them didn't turn to look at each other and just concentrated on looking out the forward glass.

"Speaking of home, I need to get to mine." Katrina said as she stood up out of the chair. "I need to get some fresh clothes and check in to work." She grabbed the bottom of his jacket she wore and tugged at it, "and I will get this washed."

"No need to hurry," Jason answered as he stood up, "let me walk you home."

"I'd like that." She smiled.

Hum* "Oooo, aren't you the gentleman."

They both ignored her and walked together down the hall and up to the door. Without any hesitation, Sheila opened the door, and they went outside. Jason and Katrina walked out of the hanger and toward her apartment.

Their conversation continued as they walked across the base. Most of it involved small talk topics like the weather, her job, his jobs, and Sheila. The in deep talk passed the time quickly and they soon found themselves in front of her complex.

The apartment that she lived in was well secured. An iron fence surrounded the front yard and in it was a large fountain with several seats around it. After entering the gate and passing the fountain, Jason and Katrina walked up to the front door. She pulled out her pass card and waved it at the sensor on the door. A buzzer sounded and the door unlocked letting them step inside. Sitting at a desk in the lobby sat a guard in his thirties. She waved at him, and he waved back. They walked to the elevator, stepped inside its open door and rode it up to the seventh floor.

Throughout the trip to her apartment, Jason kept asking her questions about her job and her hobbies. He found out that she was the Executive Communications Director of the main tower in

Serin Base. She handled all training, scheduling, ordering and inventories for all the personal in the tower and the pilots involved. She had been with Preedom for 9 cycles and was very proud of her achievements. He found her not only very intelligent but very attractive. He felt so comfortable with her, even though he'd only known her for one day, and looked forward in seeing her again.

When they reached the seventh floor, they turned left and proceeded down the hall. Four doors later, they stopped at apartment seventy-eight. She unlocked the door, but didn't step inside.

"I can't begin to tell you what you mean to me and what you've done. I'd love to ask you in but my place is a real mess." She laughed, "but I would like to make you dinner tomorrow night if you're interested?"

"I would like that very much. At least I know how to get here." He replied.

"I also probably have a lot of work waiting for me at the tower. If we can make it later in the evening, that would be great. How can I contact you?"

"Just contact me at the hotel, room forty-one." Jason said as he leaned against the wall. "Since you have to work tomorrow, that should give me plenty of time to go pick up Hawk on Tego. It's a short run, so I'll have plenty of time to get ready when I return."

"Then I'll see you tomorrow," she said stepping toward him. She leaned over and kissed him on the cheek, "goodnight."

"Goodnight' he said with a smile as the door lightly closed.

CHAPTER 7

After leaving Katrina's apartment, Jason went to "Little Chicago". He was just itching to tell someone about what happened the night before, and he couldn't wait the distance to Tego to tell Hawk, so Steve was the next target. When he arrived, he had to use his key to get in, because the bar wasn't open for another couple of hours. Because he and Hawk were silent partners for the business, he had a key to admit himself.

Steve was at the bar, with a clip board in his hand, taking inventory of his stock. The bar lights were turned all the way up because it was easier for Steve to count, but harder on his eyes. When Earth exploded, the blast burned the retinas in Steve's eyes leaving him with visual problems. He had to wear special tinted glasses almost all the time to be able to see, bright light still clouded his vision, but sometimes he could take them off. It all depended upon the level of the light. The bar was always dimmer during the shows, and of course, at night when the sun was gone. Today was no exception for he was wearing the pair now.

"Steve! You would not believe my last fourteen hours!" Jason yelled excitedly while sitting at a stool at the bar.

"Let me guess," Steve said while setting the clip board down, "Something to do with Sheila?"

"No, it started after I left the hotel...."

****

Serin base tower was always busy. It took thirty-five people to keep the daily operations going. Radio control techs, communicator operators, crop schedulers, ship loaders, landing controllers and data programmers were just a few positions that kept production going. Katrina was in charge of them all. Vegetables and spices of several varieties were needed on the other five planets and needed fast, so if one ship was off schedule, the whole day was out of order. Each ship would land, pay their wages, get loaded up and depart within a given time.

The tower itself was a large oval window that oversaw the entire port. It was located in the middle of the landing field and had a full view of the field in all directions. Entrance was at the base where armed guards conducted security checks before anyone could enter the building. Once inside the elevator, it was a straight twenty stories up to the control tower itself. Other offices and rooms were within the building, but the main control was in the tower.

Katrina had already cleared security and was riding up in the elevator. She felt warm inside with the thoughts of Jason and how she couldn't wait to see him again. Hopefully his run to Tego wouldn't take too long, but all the same it gave her more time to get the place ready. Her head still throbbed under the fresh bandages and she saw a few bruises in the mirror especially the bruise on her knee. Thanks a lot, Sheila.

The elevator door opened up and the usual noise of the tower assaulted her. She walked straight to her office on the left, grabbing the daily report chart off the door as she walked in. It was thicker than usual. She stopped, faced her desk, and sighed. She was still thinking about the night before. A tall brunette walked in and broke her concentration.

"Well, well, well where have we been young lady?" asked the girl.

Katrina turned to face her assistant.

"OH, MY WORD!" the girl exclaimed as she rushed forward to comfort her, "What happened? Kat, are you ok?"

Katrina walked around her desk and sat into her chair. "Careese, you will not believe what happened to me the last 24 courses. Have a seat, and I'll tell you."

Careese grabbed one of the other chairs and swung it in front of her desk. "Are you ok, you look terrible!"

"First things first," Katrina sighed. "What reports have I missed, and what needs to be done?"

"Are you kidding me?' asked the girl angrily. "That should be the last thing you should worry about. Kyler and I have got everything in control. When you contacted us this morning and told us you had an emergency, we just took over the daily reports."

"Thanks," Katrina smiled.

"Besides," Careese added, "you are the biggest workaholic I know. You never take days off, you never take a vacation, hell, I can't even get you out to a bar to meet someone. So, you miss a course, so what. Now what happened?"

"A man saved my life last night."

"What? How? Where?"

"Get us some Kedy brew, and I'll tell you the whole story"

Careese left the room in a hurry.

****

After leaving "Little Chicago", Jason went straight to Sheila to depart. He was sitting on her bridge, feet propped up on the counter and drinking a sizzler five. His thoughts were drifting to Katrina and her blushing smile. He could......

Hum* "Are you ready to go, or what? I've been dying to get out of this hanger for a week."

"Yes, anytime you're ready," he said snapping out of his daydream, "at least it's nice to know that we own this hanger. It would be a bitch to constantly have to find a different spot every time we returned," Jason said, taking a sip from his glass.

Hum* "Speaking of 'Bitch', you're not getting attached to the lady, are you?"

"Please don't call her that."

Hum* "Ok, fine, sorry, but are you?"

"Why not? She's intelligent, honest, shy, and very attractive."

Hum* "Not to mention gassy, did you smell that one she ripped off?"

Jason crinkled his nose, "it can happen to anyone. At least it wasn't out loud, that would have been really embarrassing."

Sheila's engines hummed to life, and she slowly slid out of the hanger scattering people on the walkway in front of her. The hanger door eased shut as she moved further down the strip. Her engines were quiet and most people couldn't hear her unless she was right up behind them. Her design was very unique.

The engine ran on solar power, and the panels comprised her entire tail assembly. The solar panels stored energy up to two weeks without having to be recharged. Her ability to fly was all controlled by small pressure pockets that worked like human pores all over her body. High compressed air when sent out at different angles and spots would move her. To make a simple turn all she had to do was release pressure on her left side, and visa- versa for the other direction. She could even move diagonally which most ships could not do.

Once she cleared the port area, she lifted up and changed her angle. Soon they were out of Largo's orbit.

Jason remained silent the entire time his thoughts drifting back to Katrina. Her face was embedded into his memory, and he could see her smile.

Hum* "Don't tell me that you're daydreaming about her again. Did she really leave that much of an impression on you?"

"Yes, she did." Jason said finishing his drink. "I don't know what it is about her, but I can't stop thinking about her."

Hum* "But you've been out with almost all the dancers at Steve's and knew them longer. Why don't you feel this way about them?"

Jason looked disgusted, "I have not been out with almost all of them, stop exaggerating."

Hum* "There's Ayela, Remy, Dresna, Matri, Aiden, Nina..."

"Oh, stop it, I flirted with a lot of them, but nothing ever became really serious. I know it's hard for you to understand, since you can't comprehend emotions, and you can only define them, but this seems different. It's like I don't want to ever see her hurt again. I never want to see her cry, and I just feel kind of empty when she is not next to me."

Hum* "Boy, have you got it bad."

"How long to Tego?" Jason said looking out the front glass.

Hum* "Oh, about an hour and a half."

"Good," Jason said leaning back in the chair. "As soon as we hit orbit, contact Hawk so we can land, pick his ass up and get back. Meanwhile, I'm going to take a nap. Wake me up when we get close."

Hum* "Good night, weirdo" she stated as the bridge lights went dark.

* * * * * * * * * *

"All I can say is WOW!" Careese smiled. "He sounds like a real gentleman, especially how he handed his jacket to you."

"I know, I feel so comfortable around him." Katrina said as she emptied her second cup of Kedy brew. "Even when he introduced me to his ship, he was very kind."

"Introduced?"

"It's a long story; it'll have to wait till later." Katrina said waving her off with her right hand. "There was one embarrassing moment though, "she added with a disgusted look on her face. "When we were alone on the bridge of his ship, he passed gas and it smelled pretty bad."

"Oh, my word," Careese said with a laugh, "he must have been embarrassed!"

"Actually, we kept on talking like it never happened."

"Well, what would one say? It wasn't out loud, was it?"

"No," she said shaking her head, "But it really smelled bad."

Careese grabbed the carafe of Kedy brew she had brought in and filled both of their mugs, "So," she pushed on, "what's the next step?"

"I'm cooking dinner for him at my apartment tonight," Katrina sighed, "and I can't wait to see him again."

"I'm so happy for you girl! All I can say is it's about time!"

Katrina glanced down at the stack of papers on her desk and sighed, "But first I've got to catch up on this mornings...."

"No, no, no, no, no!" Careese interrupted slapping her hand down on the stack, "You'll do no such thing. In your condition, you're taking the rest of the day off and possibly tomorrow as well."

"I can't do that, tomorrows a field inspection and…"

"NO! You will go home," Careese yelled as she pushed the intercom on Katrina's desk, "Kyler, get in here, I need your help."

"Coming", the speaker resounded with the man's voice.

"Look, Careese, thanks for your concern but…"

"But nothing," she said standing up as a tall man stepped into the door way.

"Holly crap," Kyler reacted, "Kat, what happened to you?"

"I'll fill you in later," Careese said pointing at Katrina, "first I need your help to get this lady to take the next couple of days off."

"I can't…" Katrina tried to speak.

"Kat, we can handle things." Careese lectured, "Your development of the daily operation schedule practically handles itself, and if there is a glitch, we can deal with it!"

"She's right," Kyler added, "even when you're not here, it's like you're holding our hands anyway."

"And as I said before," Careese spoke as she counted on her fingers, "You NEVER take a vacation and you NEVER take a personal day, hell, I can't remember you ever being sick. You've earned this!"

"I guess you're right." Katrina sighed.

"Besides," Kyler added, "If you disagree, I can always carry your ass out of the building. You know I can do it!"

Katrina smiled. "You guys are the best." She looked at Careese, then at the paperwork, then at Kyler. "Fine, I'll take the rest of the day and tomorrow off, but on the next rotation, I'll be here. It's almost the end of the inventory cycle, and I want everything to be accurate."

"Yes, boss," the other two answered in sync.

****

Sheila's engines cut back as she broke through Tego's atmosphere and started to scan for Hawk's implant. It didn't take her long to locate him in the Rayseen District. She radio contacted a hanger landing nearest his location and began her descent.

Hum* "Jason, sugar, sweetie, numb nuts, we're landing."

Jason stretched his arms as the lights slowly re-lit on the bridge. They were landing on the night side of Tego and it was very dark outside. Jason stood up and glanced out the window. Many colored lights flickered on the planet reminding him of Las Vegas.

"Did you find Hawk?"

Hum* "Yes, he's in the Rayseen district at the Crustacean. I've already made arrangements to park in Skystreet station just a few blocks down."

"Great", Jason said as he walked down the hall, "I'm going to the bathroom. Once I find him and get his stuff, we're leaving."

Hum* "Alright, Romeo, I'll tell you if he leaves the building."

Within the next twenty minutes, Jason found himself walking toward the Crustacean on a walkway he was all too familiar with. The lights, sounds and voices always made him feel like he was in an amusement park waiting for the next ride. They lived in Rayseen for over two years and always had something to do. This place was never boring, like Largo. The warm climate of the area played with his senses for he was almost used to the Largo chill. The air was also so humid that it reminded him of the heat units between the doors at the Hotel.

He arrived at the Crustacean and opened the door into a noise of gambling machines and chatter. Buzzers, lights, clinking glasses and laughter all together defined the word money. Loud cheers came from the center gambling table where he could see a person, with their back toward him, dressed in a brown leather jacket with a pair of wings embroidered on it. He started to approach this person when lot of people cussed, jeered and threw down their winnings and walked away. The person in the jacket reached down and scooped up a large pile of rolets off the table and turned quickly, almost running into him. It was Hawk.

"Hey! Jason," Hawk said as he collected his winning off of the table, "what's up?"

"Nice, jacket." Jason said as he tilted his head.

"Great, isn't it? I had made at Yemond's."

Hum* "I can't wait to see it."

"Sheila says she can't wait to see it." Jason repeated.

"Hello, little lady," Hawk said talking to Sheila through Jason, "How's my gal?"

"Recently," Jason answered, "she's being a pain the ass."

Hum* 'Hey! I resemble that remark!"

Jason shook his head. "Let's go get your stuff; I want to get back to Largo."

"Largo? Why?" Hawk bellowed as he stuffed what rolets he could into pockets. "Don't you want to have a few drinks and gamble a while? I could get Yemond to make you one of these jackets!"

"No thanks," Jason said while grabbing Hawk's left elbow, "I'll explain why on the way to your room."

"House," he said with a grin, "I bought a house."

"What?"

"I had the money, so I figured what the hell."

"Well fine," Jason said pulling him toward the exit, "I'll explain on the way to your house then."

****

After several arguments with her coworkers, Katrina was only allowed to leave if she didn't take any work home. She finally agreed and found herself walking toward her favorite Market store, the 'Harvester.' A very old and dear friend of hers, Emmatt, has owned and ran that store as long as she can remember. Through the cycles she's been there for advice, comfort, laughs and a shoulder to cry on. Katrina bought all her food from her only. The store was between the Tower and her apartment so she visited it frequently.

As she stepped into the door, Emmatt, who was watering the vegetables, saw her condition and immediately responded.

"Kat, what ever happened to you, Honey? Come here sweetie and sit down," she said pulling a chair out from behind the counter.

"Last night I got mugged."

"What? Are you ok? "She knelt down to her side and then she reached up with her hand and brushed aside Katrina's hair from the bandage, "Oh that's a nasty bruise. What a terrible thing to happen."

"Actually, "Katrina smiled, "It was the best thing that ever happened to me."

"Ok, child, you're going to have to explain this one to me." She said standing up.

"Let's just start by telling me what you would recommend for a romantic dinner?"

Emmatt's eyes glistened with hope. "Why that is good news, fill me in the details, sugar, while I get another chair and a cup of hot speckle tea for both of us."

****

Hawk's house was amazingly huge. As they pulled up the drive, a house servant opened the door for them as they entered. "I've got to show you around!" Hawk said excitedly.

"No time," Jason said pausing in the front foyer, "I want to get back as soon as possible."

"Come on, Jason, at least see the bar."

"Ok, one quick glance, and we're out of here."

They walked down a main hallway that was lined in mirrors and into a large open room with a window that oversaw the beach. As they stepped into the room, a lot of screeches almost broke Jason's ear drums as he watched five Trills run out toward Hawk.

"My babies!" he yelled as he knelt down to them, and they all started to hop all over him

"Is five all?" Jason asked, "Last time you had eight!"

"Yeah, but I decided to try some other games. Have you ever tried Iron Boxing?"

"Are you crazy?" Jason snapped, "Boxing against a robot isn't my idea of fun, it's more like self-inflicted pain."

"I won about three of those," he said as he picked up the only green Trill in the pack. Hawk started to rub its front torso and it started to purr very loud. "I'm keeping this one, he's special, and the other ones are being set free."

Hum* "He's not bringing that thing aboard me! No pet stains on my carpet!"

"Sheila says no." Jason repeated.

"Aw, come on Sheila, the trip is only a couple of hours, and he is trained. I swear anything he ruins I'll replace."

Hum* "Even the smell?"

"Even the smell," Jason repeated.

"Yes," Hawk answered.

Hum* "That's better than the other smell that we had in here yesterday..."

"Ok, knock it off." Jason growled. "Come on, Hawk, get your shit together and let's go. I want to get back!"

"Alright, I'm running. Sheesh, I never thought you'd go this crazy for a woman."

"Yeah," Jason smiled, "me neither."

****

Many miles from Serin Base were the Ashton Mountains. It was one of the most beautiful landmarks that Largo had. It was full of trees, caves and wildlife which was completely untouched by civilization. Many laws protected the wildlife and the surrounding land. The Lagrona River wound through the valley and several waterfalls added to its splendor. Unfortunately hidden in all this beauty was a dark secret. In one of the largest caves on the far lower range was a military base. Many of the men had been here for months and several years of planning brought them to this stage. All their training and preparations now came down to this moment. They had just received the final instruction to put the plan into action. The most crucial maneuver was to be implemented by the top three specialists and all the others had their assignments as well. Everything had to be timed exactly or the plan would fail.

Several rumbles of engines broke the silence in the valley and scattered Fana birds in all directions. Six ships exited the cave and went different directions, the largest one headed toward Serin Base.

CHAPTER 8

It didn't take long for Sheila to return to Largo because Jason kept pushing the issue of time. He didn't even have any drinks on the way back, although Hawk had three. Jason kept filling in every detail he could remember about Katrina to Hawk and Sheila would add in her usual comments. Just before they started to enter the atmosphere, Hawk excitedly jumped up.

"OH! I almost forgot," he yelled, running over to his stack of belongings and grabbing a large box. "Guess what I picked up at Foscal's?"

Hum* "A fire extinguisher for Jason's bad habit?"

"No," Hawk said lifting out a big electronic device out of the box, "A particle transfer unit."

"What?" Jason said getting out of his chair, "Those things are very hard to find. How'd Foscal get it?"

"He bought the spec sheet from someone and built it himself."

"But does it work, can it transfer?" Jason said taking it away from him and looking it over.

"Yes, it does."

Hum* "Bullshit."

"Bullshit," Jason repeated. "Is that what Foscal told you?"

"No, IT WORKS! I tell you," Hawk tried to convince them. "I saw him transfer one of the Trills from the bar to the outside pool!"

"What are you planning to do with it?"

"Well, I thought, wouldn't it be cool if......."

Hum* "OH, no, you're not using me as a guinea pig. I still remember when you tried to install that tracker beam on me and everything in the hanger magnetized to me."

"Come on; just think what fun you could have transferring things from one place to another." Hawk pushed for the thrill. "You wouldn't have to land anymore; you could just transfer us to a place."

Hum* "I could transfer anything, like annoying people?"

"It works on anything," Hawk stated, "just got to figure out its matrix."

"What kind of range does it have?" Jason said as he put it back in the box.

"From what he says, about ten specks, but after that, things get a little distorted."

Hum* "That wouldn't be fun, as you say, if you ended up distorted. It could kill you. Even if you say this thing does work, where would you place it? What circuit would you operate it from?"

"I'd have to crawl into you and figure that one out. I could work on it as soon as we land. Jason's got plans, and it'll give me something to do while he's out and about."

Hum* "You mean out and in and out and in and out and …."

"Stop, it." Jason snapped.

"So how about it?" Hawk asked again.

Hum* "Ok, hot shot, go ahead and give it a try. I always enjoy it when you get inside me."

Both Jason and Hawk grimaced at the sexual innuendo of the comment. Looking out the window they saw Serin Base's landing area, and Sheila banked to the left toward hanger thirty-seven. Hawk went to the back kitchen area and opened up a cabinet containing an equipment bag as Jason started walking toward the back, getting ready to exit.

Hum* "Jason, darling, want some advice?"

"From you, ha, that's a laugh."

Hum* "Honest."

"Ok, what?"

Hum* "Leave that stupid pipe in here. It's disgusting, smelly, nasty and not very attractive."

Jason pulled the pipe out of his pocket and looked it over, "You really think so?"

Hawk stuck his head out of the kitchen and nodded in agreement with Sheila. "It just doesn't fit you."

Jason looked at it again, opened up the compacter door in the hallway and tossed the pipe into it. "Ok, that's done and over with."

Instant grinding noises told them that Sheila disintegrated it.

Hum* "Good boy," she stated as the door opened with a hiss, "Now go get some poon tang!"

"Funny," Jason responded, "not yet. First, I'm going to the hotel to clean up and wait for her call." He waved his right hand in the air, "See you all, whenever!" Jason said as he exited out the door and walked out of the hanger.

"Wow, he has it bad, doesn't he," Hawk said opening the closet hall door and letting out the green Trill. "Come on baby!"

The trill screeched excitably and followed Hawk up to the bridge. When he sat in the chair, the Trill jumped into his lap and curled up.

Hum* "I know, he does have it bad. I hope he doesn't get hurt like the one two years ago. It took him forever to get over her. And don't let that thing shit on my carpet!"

"He won't." Hawk snapped back. "And about this woman, something seems different. She doesn't sound like one of the regular ones that Jason usually winds up with."

Hum* "True, she didn't start off by doing a lap dance on him."

Hawk propped his feet up on the counter, "Now, make me another Sizzler five and fill me in on everything Jason DIDN'T tell me about her."

Hum* "No problem, but first I've got to tell you what I did," she said as a drink slid out from the wall. "This is going to go down as one of the best practical jokes I've ever done."

"What did you do?" Hawk said as he grabbed the drink and then the shelf retracted back into the wall.

Hum* "When they were sitting in the bridge together yesterday, I vented the sanitary system through the fresh air conduit. You should have seen their faces when they thought each other had farted!"

Hawk started laughing out loud and almost made his drink come out of his nose. "That's cruel but very funny. I'd have to admit, it is one of your better ones." Hawk then looked concerned, "You did shut off Jason's connection so he can't hear all of this?"

Hum* "Do you think I'm that stupid? I shut it off when he stepped out the door."

"Great." Hawk said as he took a sip, "Now give me all the juicy gossip."

Hum* "With pleasure."

****

As Jason stepped into the Grand Gate Hotel, the front desk clerk waved at him. It was the same woman that he had left the large tip and he approached the counter to find out what she wanted.

"Yes?" he said quizzically looking at her.

"Good evening, sir," she said with a smile, "I just wanted to tell you that you had a visitor about a course ago. "

"Did she leave a message?"

"Not she, sir," she said shaking her head, "He. And he wasn't much of a gentleman either. He was very rude. "

"What did he want, did he leave a name?"

"No name, just asked if you were here, and I informed him that you were out. Then he left."

"Ok, interesting." Jason said rubbing his chin. "I'll be in my room, and I'm expecting a very important call. Please forward it to me as soon as you get it."

"Sure thing, Mr. Powell."

Jason turned and headed toward the elevator. He started to feel like a kid again waiting for that special surprise under the Christmas tree. If only he didn't feel so nervous about it. It's only going to be a dinner; he tried to tell himself, nothing more. He always tried to overestimate the situation and end up getting hurt. 'I just want to be friends,' was the cruelest thing anyone could say to a heart that was in love.

The elevator's ride was longer than usual because every button on the panel had been pushed. The added soft music on the speakers didn't help the situation either. He started to remember a love he had two years ago. Her name was Oleana, and she was younger than him and a dancer he met at Steve's. They were together all the time. Not only was the sex good, but they always had a good time no matter what they did. Then, because of Sheila, he found out that she was married and just stringing him along for the ride. He was like a puppet she pulled out of her closet anytime she wanted to get away from her reality. Everything he ever hoped for in that future came crashing down hard. When he confronted her about it, she got mad and stormed out of Little Chicago, and he never saw her again.

The dinging of the elevator opening broke his concentration and he walked onto the fourth floor. He started walking down the hall trying to recover from his thoughts, trying to shake doubts from his mind. As he approached the door, he could hear the call center ringing inside the room, so he quickly slid his key card on the entry pad and ran in and picked up the receiver

"Hello?" he said out of breath.

"Hey, Jason, it's Hawk."

"I just left you! What do you want?"

"Just letting you know that I shut down Sheila's power. I didn't want to fry my ass while I was up inside her, and besides, I figured you could use the break tonight."

"Thank you SOOOO much, Drinks are on me next time we're at Steve's."

"We get all our drinks free anyway, fool, I'll catch up with ya later, good luck. AND TAKE IT SLOW!"

"I hear ya, "Jason said putting down the receiver, "I hear ya."

After closing off the vid receiver, Jason started to get himself ready. He got out fresh clothes, took a shower, freshened up his hair and put on some cologne. Once he was dressed, he relaxed in the recliner waiting for the call. He started flipping through the channel selector on the vid screen and didn't really see anything he wanted to watch. He laughed to himself about how on Earth, you had a satellite reception that could offer over hundreds of channels, but could never find anything to watch either. Nothing seemed interesting. The same outcome was here as well, nothing.

Suddenly, the call vid toned, he reached over and picked up the receiver.

"Hello?"

"Jason," said her voice.

Hearing her sent warm sensations across his shoulders and down his back. His ears also seem to warm up with the touch of her voice. "Hello, Katrina. How was the rest of your day?"

"Very productive, are you ready for dinner?"

"Yes," he said a little too fast.

"I hope you like spicy food,"

"I adore spicy food. In fact, I haven't found anything that's too hot for me yet!"

"Great, I'll start cooking it."

"I'll be there in ten taps."

"I'll be waiting."

He set down the receiver and immediately jumped up from the chair. He proceeded to the bathroom and looked into the mirror, expecting to see something that needed fixing. He ran his comb through his brown hair again making sure it looked perfect. Leaning forward he looked deep into the mirror at his face. Wrinkles were becoming more noticeable and a couple of spots were there that didn't used to be there.

"What's wrong with me," he said out loud. "I feel jittery, nervous and very scared about this. Why am I trembling? Could this end up to be something or am I just wishful thinking again?"

When the face in the mirror didn't answer back, he turned and left the bathroom. On the way past the front room, he grabbed his brown coat off of the couch, put it on, and left the hotel room.

From the hall and into the elevator, his nervousness persisted. His mind kept bringing up her voice, her hair, her eyes, her height, her softness of her skin and even the way her cheek puffed out when she chewed her food. He just couldn't stop thinking about her every move. He couldn't be falling in love with her, not this quick, but what else could it be? He started thinking about all the girls that Sheila had listed yesterday and none of them brought on the sensation that Katrina did. The last time he felt this way was two years ago with Oleana. Suddenly his warm sensation turned to a cold chill running down his back as he thought about the pain. It was crazy what a broken heart can do to you. It turned him into a hermit who only sat in the corner at Steve's, drinking his life away. Hawk and Steve tried everything to shake him out of it. He didn't want to have anything to do with anyone. He turned rude to some of the dancers and lost his ability to do something for himself. Life didn't seem like a reason to get excited about anymore. Maybe that explained why he was so nervous; he didn't want to have the pain again.

Shaking off the past and refocusing on his present, Jason exited the elevator and walked through the lobby. It was extra crowded today; a lot of pilots could be seen in their flight gear. He excused himself through the crowd and exited the Hotel.

His nervousness continued as he proceeded toward her apartment. His mind raced of the possibilities and his next step to take. Would it be good? Would it be bad? What if she ends up being different? What if she was a lousy cook? What if....

"Jason, stop it!" He yelled out loud to himself. "Stop 'ifing' yourself to death." His frustration with himself took up all the time to get to her place and he found himself at the front entrance.

The chime on the door made her jump with excitement. She took off the apron she had on and laid it on the kitchen counter. She felt scared, jittery, and very nervous. She couldn't stop thinking about him. The way his hair looked, his voice, his eyes, the gentle touch of his hand and the way he held his fork when he ate. She could never find the time to meet someone, for work owned her, and she barely had time to sleep and eat. Something about last night woke her up. It told her that life was too short and nobody should cut themselves short. Life was meant to be joyous, happy and fun.

She ran to the door, stopped, ran her hands down her dress to flatten out the wrinkles and then opened the door.

There he stood, dressed in a brown jacket and dark blue pants. He looked so handsome and she lit up with energy just seeing him.

"Something smells good!" he said with widened eyes.

"Please, come in," she said waving him in.

She was gorgeous. He glanced at her light-yellow dress which hung just a little below her knees and was decorated with flower patterns. It was tied up on her shoulders in big bows and had a low-cut front. She wore a gold necklace which stood out on her upper chest and it sparkled in the light. Her face glowed with radiance and seemed to brighten up the entire room.

"Let me have your jacket," she said holding out her hand. Jason took off his jacket and she saw that he was wearing a maroon sweater which made her heart race. It happened to be her favorite color, and he looked very good in it.

"Dinner's almost ready," she said as she walked the coat toward the closet on the right and hung it up. "Please, make yourself at home." she gestured toward the couch in the front room.

The smell of dinner teased his nose with senses of spice and flavor. He could almost taste it in the air. As he stepped into the living room, he looked at its contents which contained a large couch centered in the room with an end table on either side. The couch faced the front wall which had a vid screen and a crackling fire going in the fireplace below it. Toward the right was an open kitchen, where Katrina was standing and an archway in the back that led to another room. To the left side was another door in the center of the wall and bookshelves on both sides of it. A lot of books and knickknacks filled the shelves.

He sat down on the couch and tensed up. He wondered if he should sit up straight or if he should lean back or…. this is ridiculous, he thought. Just be myself. There is no reason to be something you're not. If she doesn't like you for you, what's the point in trying? His mind started to race again, and he told himself to slow down.

"So, when am I going to meet Hawk?" she said from the kitchen.

"Didn't really think about it, but you'll see him soon enough. He's working on putting a new unit into Sheila, which by the way is shut off."

"You mean she's not going to be with us?" Katrina smiled

"Not for a while, at least."

Katrina got a glow in her eyes, "It'll be like the parents leaving the children home alone, then"

"When the cat is away, the mice will play." Jason smirked.

Katrina laughed, "The what and the who?"

"Never mind," he said.

"Well, if you're ready," she said lifting up a large bowl, "Follow me into the dining room and let's eat."

Jason followed behind her as she entered the room next to the kitchen.

****

Hawk was frustrated. The unit would fit with no problem but he couldn't get the wiring right and it kept burning circuits. He was all the way up into Sheila's tail assembly, which was only four feet wide and fifteen feet long, and it was getting hot. Sweat was pouring off his forehead and stinging his eyes. He guessed that he had been working on her for almost three courses and he was at a giving up point. He was satisfied about the location of the unit, but he thought it would be a good idea to stop before he lost his temper. That's when he decided that enough was enough and started to slither out backwards. Just before he stepped down on the extruding ladder, he flipped on a power switch that was right next to a rusted plaque. The plaque read 'Zenith Eclectic Universal System'.

As he jumped down, Sheila's ladder retracted into the tail end.

"I'm going to Little Chicago to clear my head and have a few drinks, talk to ya later." He then walked out of the hanger and down the walkway and never noticed that she didn't answer.

****

The dining room table candles were half the size from when they started dinner. The meal consisted of Mechay Salad, string Rupa and Spiced Guna steak which melted in your mouth. It all was very delicious. During their entire dinner, they got to know more about each other better.

Katrina was a native to Largo and never had been off planet. She was an orphan, and never knew her real parents because they left her at a local hospital only when she was six months old. She couldn't understand why anyone would give up on a child, no matter what the circumstances. She was raised on a farm in a small town called Greenston, and graduated from TechConn with an Electronic Operative Disparge, equivalent to what Jason knew as a Master's Degree. Her experience in the farming and the training she had with TechConn landed her a job with Preedom about two courses later and now she was in charge of the main tower. She loved to watch documentaries on the Vid and loved to cook, as Jason found out. She had two really good friends; Careese and Emmatt whom she planned to introduce them as soon as she could.

Jason was more reserved about his past. He had lived on Tego for about two cycles and ran a gambling casino with an old friend named Rodger. After leaving there, he moved to Serin base. His next venture was to help a friend, named Steve, build a night club called "Little Chicago." in which Hawk and he were silent partners. She knew about the place, Careese tried to get her to go several times but outside of that, Jason was not all open about his past.

They decided to take their glasses of Berkley wine into the living room to talk more. As Katrina walked into the kitchen to refill her glass, Jason walked over toward the book shelves at the other side of the room.

"I see you love to read," he said glancing at the first book tower on the left, "what's your favorite genre?"

"I'm a big fan of documentaries and travel guides. I'm just a walking encyclopedia when it comes to history and facts," she said as she filled up her glass and re plugged the bottle.

Jason moved onto the second tower on the opposite side of the door frame. He saw that many of the books were old and torn. Then something caught his eye; a faded blue binder that was about two inches thick. He reached up and slowly pulled it out as Katrina walked across the room up to him. She didn't notice his blank expression when she saw what book he had, but knew the book well.

EARTH-A WORLD OF PROGRESS AND TECHNOLOGY
By M.R. MORELLI

"I've had that book ever since I was a kid," she said laughing. "I never returned it to Serin Base library. Somewhere there is probably a large fine waiting for me."

Jason suddenly got a chill over the back of his neck, "How in the world did this, where did...."

"Jason," she said quizzically, "what's wrong?"

He slowly walked over to the couch, with the book in his hand, and sat down. "How did this get here? Who could have...." he said as he drifted off.

Katrina walked over to him and sat next to him. She put her hand on his, "Jason, What's wrong?"

He looked up slowly at her, "I'm from Earth."

Katrina's eyes widened, "Really? Wow?" she said excitedly. "What can you tell me about it? I could never find any other books about it. I must have read that book at least three times. A lot of its culture and beauty inspired me to understand that life didn't end with Largo."

Jason remained silent.

"Well, tell me all about it," she said as she took the book out of his hand, "I'm dying to learn more. Perhaps you can take me there and show me around." That's when she noticed the tear running down Jason's face.

"Jason, what's wrong?"

"Earth is gone," he said coldly.

Katrina's expression turned to sadness, "What do you mean gone? How?"

"It was blown up by greedy power-hungry individuals. Steve, Rodger and I are the only survivors."

"What? You're the only ones to survive?"

"At the time, I was in the army. Rodger and I were assigned to guard a special operation unit, you know her as Sheila, but at that time she was known as ZEUS."

Katrina nodded her head, "The Zenith Eclectic Universal System?"

Jason's eyes glazed over. "Yes," he said surprised by her knowledge. "If it wasn't for her, or him, we wouldn't have survived."

Katrina walked around the back side of the couch, behind Jason, and started to massage his shoulders. Jason tensed up.

"I'm so sorry to hear about this." she said as she gently rubbed his shoulders, "I can't imagine the pain you are going through. I had the pain of never knowing my parents, but you lost everyone you knew"

Jason sighed from her touch, "It took a while for all three of us to live with it. We all lost families. I can still remember going out to the lake in my hometown of Taylorville, Illinois. Lots of memories at that place..." Another tear fell down his cheek, for thoughts of Thanksgiving's at his grandmother's house flooded him with many memories. His Grandmother always made the best homemade egg noodles.

"How long where you out in space?" Katrina asked.

"About three months, or I mean three terms but thanks to Zeus' ability to search space grids for information, he found this system."

Her heart started to warm up with a burning sensation. As she massaged his shoulders, she could feel his tenseness starting to relax. This man, who seemed so invincible the other night, now is so very fragile. She walked back toward the front of the couch and knelt down in front of him. She put her arms on his legs and rested her head on top of her arms.

"Jason, I think I'm falling in love with you," she whispered while rubbing his knee.

There it was that word again. The word that set Jason off into dream lands of happiness and fantasy and later come back to crush his soul. He has been told this before, but with terrible endings. How was he supposed to accept it? Rush into her arms or tense up into a closed shell. Was he ready to get hurt again or could this possibly be the real thing?

Hum* "Oh, God, I can't stand it anymore! I can't keep quiet!"

Jason's expression changed to anger. "How long have you been listening?"

Katrina's face acknowledged that she knew Sheila was talking.

Hum* "I've been on for about a half an hour now and wow can she work you! I'm recording all of this for future use, when you get hurt again."

"YOU WOULDN'T DARE." Jason yelled.

Katrina responded angrily, "What she doing?"
"She's recording the whole conversation." Jason said in frustration.

Anger masked Katrina's face briefly but then she began to smile. Getting up off her knees, she stood in front of Jason and bent over to him.

"Sheila," Katrina whispered, "Record this." She leaned forward toward Jason and cupped his head into her hands. Their lips got closer and closer to each other and just before they touched, Katrina pushed the button.

****

Hawk walked into Little Chicago with only one thing in mind, to get drunk. His frustration with the transfer unit had him so tense that he just wanted to relax for the rest of the night. Seeing Steve at the bar, he walked up to an open stool, sat down and slammed his fists on the counter.

"Hey," Hawk yelled, "how about some service over here?"

Steve turned with an angry look that quickly turned a large grin on his face, "Well, young man, good to see you." Steve held out his hand which Hawk graciously shook.

"Got anything new to try?'

"Got just the thing for ya," Steve answered as he reached for a bottle that was hidden in a cabinet. "It's called the flame thrower."

"Pour me up one in a number six; I plan to be here all night." Hawk scooted the bar stool closer to the counter.

"Did you just get in?" Steve said as he fixed the drink in the mixer.

"No, been here for about three courses working on Sheila."

"What's wrong with her, besides her attitude, of course?"

"I got a hold of a Particle Transfer unit and can't seem to get it installed without blowing half the system. Can't figure out the dynamics, and I'm furious."

"Well, you couldn't have come to a better place to relax." Steve propped his elbows on the counter, "I've got a new singing group playing tonight from Tego. The lead singer has a hell of a voice. I heard the audition tapes and hired them. They should be arriving within the course to set up."

"Sounds good to me, I plan to stay here all night, might as well get some entertainment out of it. I'll go sit at Jason's usual table." Hawk said while getting off the stool

"That table is going to be their VIP table, so we can get to know them better. Is Jason coming in later?"

Hawk smiled, "I highly doubt it."

****

The bedroom was cool and inviting when they entered kicking off their shoes. Still engaged in a passionate kiss, he had his hands around her head and she held tight around his waist as they walked up to the side of the bed. When their lips released, she slowly pulled his sweater up and off his body. His chest showed very little hair and his muscles were very tight. She started rubbing his chest with her hands, around his dog tags, as he started untying the left strap of her dress on her shoulder. When it was undone, he moved to right shoulder and untied the last strap as she continued to caress is chest. When the strap was undone, she lightly wiggled her body allowing the dress to fall to the floor. She was braless and stood in front of him with only light-yellow panties. The lights in the room glistened off her breasts and her nipples stood very erect from the cool chill of the air. She moved her hands from his chest and down to his belt buckle and started to unfasten it. He started unbuckling his holster belt. When both belts were removed, they were thrown into the chair next to the bed. She then unsnapped his pants and slowly pulled down the zipper as he lightly fondled her bare shoulders. When his pants fell to the floor, he stepped out of them and they both fell onto the cool touch of the bed's comforter.

Lying side by side, they started to kiss again as he slowly caressed the bottom of her left breast. He lightly touched it with the tips of his fingers, doing little circles, and slowly worked his way to the center. Closer and closer he came to the nipple, but he never touched it. He circled around it with one fingertip, then worked his way back out to the lower part again. He repeated the circular movement again but this time he very lightly brushed across the nipple which made her release a long stuttering sigh.

Their hands caressed each other's curves as she slowly rubbed his back and shoulders. Her touch made him shiver with excitement.

His kiss moved from her lips down to her right breast as he lightly licked it with his tongue. He put the nipple into his mouth, very gently, and rolled it around with his tongue. When he released it, he blew on it with a light breath and it made it stiffen up even harder. She squirmed at his touch and moaned with each lick. He then moved to the other breast and repeated the same moves.

Katrina kept running her fingers through his hair and lightly massaged his scalp. She closed her eyes and her breathing became short bursts from her mouth.

He then worked his mouth up to her left ear and started to nibble on it. The sensation made her shudder uncontrollably and she let out a cry. He reached down below her waist and started pulling off her panties. She lifted up her legs and with her toes, pulled them off and tossed them to the side. He pulled off his briefs and threw them to the floor.

Once again, his hands started massaging her breasts then slowly worked down to her belly. When he stuck his finger into her belly button, she giggled. Using the one finger tip, he then worked circles down past her belly and down between her legs lightly caressing her. She wiggled as the feeling was exhilarating, adding to her already heightened state. He moved faster and faster to the point where she tilted back her head and started taking short breaths of air. She flung her arms out to the sides, and her fingers wiggled.

He then stopped nibbling on her ear and started licking the inside of it which made her tremble with a gasp. Quicker and quicker, he touched her and she could not restrain herself anymore. She tilted her head back again and let out a cry of excitement. She brought her hands back to his shoulder length hair as he rolled over on top of her.

Then, he slowly slid into her.

The sensation jolted her to extreme ecstasy. She lowered her hands from his hair and onto his back, feeling the sweat all over him. She caressed him as he raised and fell again and again giving her an overpowering joy. The motion between their bodies was building heat as they both reached emotional exaltation. Warmer and warmer their bodies grew as he continued to penetrate her.

His breathing in her ear made her reach a delight she had never experienced. The activity was building her up to an emotional burst. Every muscle in her body trembled as they both reached a climatic peak.

She screamed loudly releasing the passion within her. He, too, yelled as well, reaching that ultimate pleasure. Their lips met again, kissing strongly and emotionally. Then he fell upon her, exhausted and out of energy. They both just laid together, their bodies wrapped around each other in a puddle of sweat and felt completely exhilarated.

The once coolness of the room was now gone and the mirror on the other side of the wall was completely fogged up.

CHAPTER 9

"Come on, grandpa," she said as she swatted him in the belly, "let's go make some drinks."

Out on the floor Katrina approached table seven. The two men were laughing at something and then stopped when she arrived. They both Later in the evening, 'Little Chicago' started to get crowded. The band that was playing tonight, The Gamblers, was well known on Tego, and it was their first performance on Largo. Steve had booked them a year in advance and paid full fee before they agreed. The stage was filled with all their instruments, and they were going to start playing any tap. The band featured three men and two women, who had been together since the group started.

Steve had every one of his employees working tonight because reservations for the evening started pouring in as soon as he advertised it. He had six people behind the bar, ten waitresses on the floor and six bouncers. Tonight, was going to bring in a lot of money. His charge for entering the door was ten rolets, double what he usually charged. After a sellout crowd, within thirty-six courses of posting it, he had already made up his cost for the band.

He planned on buying all the drinks for the band as well and had food sitting on a table behind the stage for them. He heard that this was one of the best bands in the system so he was going to sit at the VIP table and enjoy the show. After double checking all the needs of the business, Steve made himself a drink and joined Hawk at the table.

"Well, this is a first," Hawk said as he saw Steve pull up a chair to his right.

"Yes, it is," he said sitting down, "I plan to enjoy this with no interruptions."

"I've never seen this band before," Hawk added, "but they sure have a reputation on Tego."

"I haven't seen them perform either, but when I heard her voice, I had to get them here."

"Mind if we join you?" asked a voice from behind them

Steve and Hawk turned and saw Jason with a woman.

"Please," Steve said as he and Hawk stood up.

"Katrina," Jason said pulling the chair to the right of Steve out for her, "I'd like you to meet two dear friends of mine. This gentleman to your left is Steve, owner of Little Chicago."

"My pleasure," he said, shaking her hand as she sat down.

"And that strapping young lad over there is Hawk," Jason added as he sat in the chair to Katrina's right.

"I've heard a lot about you," Hawk said reaching across the table for a shake.

"I hope good things," she smiled.

"I'm, surprised to see you two here," Hawk added with a smile.

"Well two things," Jason said, "number one I've seen this band and they are fantastic, I couldn't pass this up. And number two, Katrina has never been to a place like this and I thought tonight would be the perfect introduction." He then turned toward Katrina and continued, "Steve alternates performances every three days. Last night was comedy night and tomorrow night will be the dance show."

"And the guy I had in here last night was hilarious. He really made you fall off your seat." Steve added.

"And speaking of seat," Jason added, "since when do you sit on your ass and with a drink as well?"

"I'm going to take the night off. I also made this table the band's VIP table and with the help of you two, I can maybe talk them into booking a few more nights with us," Steve stated while taking a drink.

A waitress walked up to the table and stood waiting for attention.

"Oh, good God," Steve said with a sigh, "What needs done now?"

"Nothing, Boss," the girl said. "I just wanted to get everyone's order."

"Yeah, relax, you slave driver," Jason said pointing at him, "Man, you're such an ass." He turned to Katrina and gestured toward the waitress, "What would you like, darling?"

"I'll take something sweet and at a low level." She said to the waitress.

"I suggest a Sunset three," the waitress offered, "and for you Jason?"

"I'll have a galaxy five."

"And you, sir?" she nodded toward Hawk.

"Make mine another Flamethrower six."

"Another Iron Fist eighteen for you, boss?"

Jason and Hawk glanced at Steve in surprise. They had never seen Steve loosen up like this before.

"That will be fine, Aiden, thanks." He then noticed the eyes at the table staring at him. "What? Hey, I said I was taking the night off."

"This is turning into a very surprising evening," Jason stated.

"Well," Hawk said, "I've got something else to surprise you about. First, I couldn't get the particle transfer unit hooked up. The wiring couldn't handle the load. I don't know if it's the system that is refusing it, or that Foscal sold me a bad unit. Second, I left Sheila off so that you two could enjoy your evening."

"Thank you," Katrina said putting her hand on top of Jason's on the table.

"And third" Hawk added as he started laughing, "Do you remember yesterday when you two thought each other farted on the bridge?"

Both Katrina and Jason got embarrassed looks on their faces which made Hawk laugh even louder. Katrina blushed. "Sheila vented the air unit from the bathroom into the bridge system to make you guys think that!"

Steve started laughing out loud, "You'll have to admit, that's one of her better tricks."

"Oh, she is so..." Jason said with a sneer.

"That really makes me..." Katrina added.

They both turned to each other and started laughing as well.

Then the lights in the bar seating area started to dim down. That's when Steve pulled out his sun glasses and put them on. The stage lights came on bright and blue as the large red curtain out front slowly rose, showing four members of the band with their instruments and another curtain between them still closed. The music started; a slow rhythm of blues brought out a hush from the crowd as a voice started to hum to the tune.

Then she walked out, all dressed in tight black leather, carrying a microphone. She had to be at least six feet tall, slender and had a very full head of red hair that streamed past her shoulders. She wore red high heels that balanced her body as a whole. She walked up to a stool that was in the center stage, sat down and began to sing;

Love is serene,
The meaning of love has lost its charm.
Love is so mean,
Just as you think you are safe from harm.
Hearts are so fake,
I'm scared that I'll never see.
Hearts tend to break,
A love that will never be.

It's always the same
I don't like the game
My long tears are for real
It's hard for me to heal
From the pain

Why do I try?
I fear to try love's grasp within.
Why do I cry?
I fear to hold someone close in.
Love is so true,

If only love would be so kind.
Love turns on you,
If only I wouldn't be so blind.

It's always the same
I don't like the game
My long tears are for real
It's hard for me to heal
From the pain

It's always the same
I don't like the game
My long tears are for real
It's hard for me to heal
From the pain

The place went crazy. People were cheering, clapping, whistling and standing. The Female singer bowed and waved her hand toward the band to her sides. Then she addressed the crowd.

"I would like to welcome you all to 'Little Chicago', here in Serin Base. We are much honored to be playing for the first time here on Largo. We are 'The Gamblers' and I'm your host Veronica, so get ready to dance the night away."

As the waitress started setting drinks down on the VIP table, everyone's thoughts were on Veronica.

What Katrina saw was a very slender attractive woman. The woman did not seem shy and looked to be very comfortable in strange surroundings. She saw an adventurer who was taking on the system and catching her dreams. This talented person wasn't afraid of letting herself go. Her job was not restricted to a building or room, but the solar system was her stage, and she looked like she enjoyed it.

What Jason saw was a very attractive lady who wore a dress that showed every bump and curve on her body. The dress was skin tight and was a one piece. It was cut short like a mini skirt and showed her shapely legs. Her red hair was flowing and looked like fire. Her lips were also red with lipstick and when she sang looked like they could talk you into anything. She was a very attractive lady indeed.

What Steve saw was lots of money in his future. She was a beautiful singer and her voice was almost hypnotic. They were going to play three sets, with a twenty-tap break between them. He had told them about the VIP table when they arrived to set up earlier today, and they accepted his invitation. She was one hell of a singer.

Hawk was in love. He had never seen someone so beautiful in his whole life. She entranced him with each word she sang and each step she took. He couldn't break eye contact with this woman. From her body shape, to her legs, to the tightness of her dress around her ass and her overall appearance, he was mesmerized. My word, she was gorgeous!

When they started to play the next song, Jason turned to Katrina. "Care to dance?"

"I don't know how," She answered.

"That's ok," Jason said standing and taking her hand, "I'll teach you."

Katrina stood up and they both walked out to the dance floor where several other couples have already gathered.

They embraced each other closely, feeling each other's warmth. He whispered in her ear that she looked very beautiful tonight and she smiled. They closed their eyes as they twirled lightly around the floor. Katrina mis stepped a couple of times but Jason helped her regain her timing. Their hearts were beating together to the rhythm of the music and it all felt so relaxing, so tranquil.

The first set ended after several fast and slow tunes and each song was rewarded with a round of applause. Jason and Katrina danced several of the songs, all the slow ones and Katrina's dancing was improving with each step. The last song of the set was an instrumental only and when it was finished, Veronica picked up the microphone.

"Thank you. We will now take our first break of the evening and be back in twenty taps." She then set the microphone on top of her stool and started walking off the stage.

Hawk started to get nervous for he saw that she was walking down the back steps and toward their table. When she approached, all three of the men stood up, and Hawk pulled out the chair to his left for her to sit down.

"Veronica," Steve said, "I'd like you to meet some friends of mine. This lady is Katrina,"

"Hello," Veronica acknowledged with a nod.

"And these two," Steve continued, "are my silent Partners. This man is Jason Powell,"

"Nice to meet you," Jason said, shaking her hand.

"And this man," Steve said, "is Hawk."

"The pleasure is mine." Hawk said lightly taking her hand. He never shook it, but it took him a while to let it go.

"Silent partners, huh?" she said as she sat down and Hawk scooted her chair in. "I like what you did to this place; it gives it a homey feeling. My apologies, but the rest of the band will not join us; they don't like to mingle with the crowd during gigs. They're quite happy with the table you provided back stage." Then she turned to Hawk, "I saw the wings on the back of your jacket, I love animals, especially ones that fly. What do those wings represent?"

"Well, actually, me," he answered with a smile on his face.

"So, you can fly?" she said sarcastically.

"I tend to soar above everyone else." He smirked.

Veronica got a half quizzical smile on her face as the waitress came to the table. "I'll have a ball breaker eleven," she said to the waitress without being asked.

"And another round for everyone," Steve added. When the waitress left with the order, Steve turned toward Veronica, "Veronica, with all of us gathered here, I thought together we'd be able to get you to set future dates for Little Chicago." Steve suggested.

"I like someone who comes straight to the point," she said smiling. "I was very surprised to see a place like this in Serin, actually. It's very inviting." She thought of the offer for a second, and then nodded her head. "I'll talk to the rest of the band later, but I have no problem with it. We're pretty much booked up for the next cycle except the next six rotations. We all decided to take a vacation when we left Tego for this place."

The waitress brought everyone's drinks to the table and Veronica downed half of hers in one gulp. "So, you three are owners, what do you do, Katrina, is it?"

"Yes," she answered. "I'm the Executive Communications Director for the Serin base port."

"Ouch, sweetie, sounds like you burn a lot of brain cells in that job. I couldn't handle the trapped feeling of being in one place all the time. Standing in one spot drives me nuts!"

"What about your job?" Katrina questioned, "All those exciting places must be fun?"

"Oh yeah, fun." Veronica said with a smirk, "To constantly move around, no place to call home, staying in dingy hotels, having creeps slobber all over you who only want to get into your pants and give you what they think is the best fuck you'll ever have," she lifted up her drink in a toast, "Oh, yeah, that's fun."

Startled Katrina said "Then why..."

"Why do I do it? Because I love to sing," she said as her face seemed to glow. "I love to perform. Music is my way of expressing my emotions. Most of my songs are written about my life and experiences." Then she leaned across the table toward Katrina, "and just for the record, there is only one pervert to every fifty decent people in these places." She lifted her glass and downed the rest of it. Then turning toward Hawk next to her and quizzically raising an eyebrow, she stated, "So which one are you, the one or the fifty?"

Hawk smiled, glanced around the table and then looked straight into Veronica's eyes, "Why, I'm a pervert."

Veronica got a smile on her face. "I like that answer," she laughed.

"You said you like it when people are straight to the point," Hawk added.

"Something tells me I'm going to see more of you," she said as she winked at him. "Well," she exclaimed as she stood up, "Time for round two." And as she left for the stage, all three men quickly stood up and then sat back down.

"Wow, "Katrina said hesitantly, "She's, a, very colorful."

"She is unique," Jason added

"She's gorgeous," Hawk sighed while watching her walk back to the stage.

Steve turned his head and patted Hawk's shoulder, "Easy there, pal, "he said, "Take a breath."

Everyone started to smile.

"Excuse me," said a man's voice behind them, "Are one of you Jason Powell?"

Jason turned toward a man standing next to the table. He was dressed in a pilot's jump suit and it was stained with grease. His hair looked like it had been dipped in a barrel of lubricating oil and he looked completely exhausted. "That would be me?" he acknowledged.

"Is it true that you do cargo runs on short notices?" Then he reached up and wiped his arm across his face and left a greasy smear.

"Yes," Jason said standing up, "Let's go back here to the office where it's a little quieter, and we can talk."

The two men left the table area and went into an archway next to the bar leaving Katrina with the others. Suddenly she realized that she was alone with two men that she hardly knew. She felt a little uncomfortable and didn't know what to say. Jason had told her a little about them but she still felt out of place, an outsider. She looked over at Steve and smiled.

"So, you run the tower?" Steve said while taking a drink.

"Yes." She answered. Then turned to look at Hawk and noticed that he never took his eyes off of Veronica. She was up on-stage getting things ready for the next set and Hawk looked like he was in a trance. Veronica moved her stool to the back of the stage and set the microphone on a stand. When she was finished, she went behind the curtain.

Steve noticed Katrina looking at Hawk in concern, "Don't mind him," Steve said pointing toward Hawk, "If he gets too out of control, I'll just use the fire extinguisher on him."

Katrina laughed.

"Good to see you're having a good time," Steve then lowered his voice, "and to let you in on a secret, Jason is very fond of you."

"I'm very fond of him too," she smiled thinking about the past rotation. "But he seems to be quite closed up about what happened in his past, you know, on Earth."

"You know about Earth?" Steve 's eyes widened.

"It's a long story, "she sighed while taking a sip of her drink. Then she leaned over to Steve, "What's his story," she whispered while pointing at Hawk, "Jason never told me his back ground."

"Now that is a long story."

"Would you mind bending my ear sometime?" she asked.

"Love to," Steve responded with the lift of his glass.

Jason returned from the back office and sat back down in his chair. "Looks like I got a run tomorrow, and getting a huge pay to do it."

"What's the job?" Hawk said snapping out of his trance.

"This guy can't get his engines fixed and he needs to deliver a medical shipment to Zeta. It's time sensitive and I've got to leave early in the morning to do it. I'm going to have to use Sheila's clamps, are they operational?"

"Oh yeah," Hawk said nodding his head and finishing his drink. His attention still drawn toward the stage, he talked to Jason without looking at him. "What's the weight?"

"She can handle it. I have the tank's location here in port and where to drop it off on Zeta. Did you want to come?"

"Ah," he said hesitantly glancing toward the stage. "No, I'd rather stay here."

Jason got the hint as he smiled. "Ok, just do me a favor and sometime tonight get that Trill out of the closet. I don't want to deal with it."

"Oh, I already put him in a pet port." Hawk answered as the lights went dim again and the stage lights came on. "Ok, Ok, hush up everyone." He said waving his hands.

Katrina, Jason and Steve all smirked at each other.

The next set was even better than the first. They started with a slow song, then picked up the pace with a fast song, and then dropped back down to slow song again. They flipped back and forth like that often giving a good mix for the crowd. A lot of couples were dancing on the floor and as Steve looked around the bar, he tried to think about when it was the last time, he saw it this crowded. Everything was moving smoothly behind the bar as well as on the floor. He couldn't wait to count sales the next morning. In fact, he wasn't planning on opening on time so that he could give the staff tonight a well-deserved rest from tonight.

The second set ended, and Veronica joined them at the table once again.

"Wow, your stage lights get hot," she said taking a drink from her glass.

"Not as hot as you," Hawk threw out.

Everyone looked surprised and shocked. Jason thought Hawk was going to blow it with that line. He remembered all the corny lines that people used in bars on Earth, and that one was one of the worst. They all held their breath waiting for the response.

"I get that comment a lot," Veronica said smiling at him.

"Even from the perverts?" Hawk questioned as he raised an eyebrow.

Veronica smiled again and leaned toward him, "You're a cute little shit," and pinched his cheek.

Everyone looked back and forth between each other except Hawk and Veronica. They looked entranced with each other. The waitress dropped off another round of drinks and everyone around the table was very quiet. Jason broke the silence.

"You said you're taking a vacation? What are your plans?"

"I really haven't thought about it," she answered turning away from Hawk and looking at Jason. "The rest of the band is planning to bar hop around, but I just don't get into that crap. I love to go sightseeing and since this is my first time here, I thought I'd look around."

Hawk bolted upright in his chair, "I'd love to give you a tour?"

Veronica's eyes turned to his, glittering. "I was hoping you were going to offer."

"Why do I feel like a fifth wheel here?" Steve threw out.

"I don't think they heard you," Jason added.

Veronica looked deep into Hawk's eyes, "you have the prettiest blue eyes I've ever seen"

"I get that comment a lot," Hawk bounced back.

Veronica laughed.

"Blue now..." Jason whispered to Steve who laughed at the comment.

"And you are the most gorgeous person I have ever met." Hawk responded.

Veronica drank down the rest of her glass and stood up. "I've got one more set and I'll be right back"

"I'll be right here," said Hawk.

Veronica left the table and headed back to the stage.

They all glanced around the table looking at each other trying to comprehend what just took place. Steve leaned over to Hawk, "Hey, Romeo, don't you're think your taking this fast?"

"Hell no," he bellowed, "Did you see the way she looks at me?"

"Looks like love at first sight," Katrina commented. "I've read a lot of stories with that, but I've never really seen it, until now."

"Disgusting, isn't it?" said Steve.

Jason laughed, "Well, I'd love to see the results of this endeavor but I've got to get Sheila ready in the morning." He turned toward Katrina, "Did you want to stay for the last set?"

"No, not really," she said rubbing her head, "The music sounds like it's pounding my head. I still feel a little sore from last night."

"Fine with me," Jason agreed, "Your place or mine?"

"Let's go to mine." She said smiling. "When you leave in the morning, I can get started on my inventory. Everything I need is already at my place, so I really don't have to take the time to dress up to go to the office. Working in a house coat is as relaxed as you can get."

Jason reached into his pocket and pulled out a key card. "Here," he said throwing it at Hawk who caught it in midair, "It's room forty-one at the Grand Gate. I'll turn Sheila back on in the morning, so we can enjoy the rest of the night." Jason said.

Both Katrina and Jason stood up out of their chairs and Katrina put her arm around Jason's arm, "Let's not waste the time alone then."

"Good luck, frisky," Jason said to Hawk who waved him off. "She might bite harder than a Trill."

"I'm counting on that," Hawk answered back.

Steve watched the two leave through the crowd as the lights came on for the next set.

After the band had finished their set, the club closed for the night. Steve had to count out all the deposits and finish the reports before he left. Veronica changed into a pair of slacks and a light blue blouse and sat at the table with Hawk. They got to know each other a little more as they waited for Steve and they talked for about twenty taps about their favorite things to do. When she found out that he knew Tego very well, they started talking about places they both enjoyed. She loved to gamble and so did he, in a different way, but what enticed her was the mystery around him. He never told her where he grew up or what things he did before meeting Jason. He would change the subject when she would ask anything about his life.

She, on the other hand, told him how she was born and raised in a club on Tego. Her parents were entertainers as well, but died in a fire when she was twenty-one. She grew up around traveling shows all her life and had seen a lot of odd things. She'd had several one-night stands and only one real serious relationship but found that the travel was too much for them. She could never really feel comfortable with anyone, but Hawk was different. In just this short time, she felt very comfortable around him and relaxed.

After Steve was finished, they all decided to get breakfast at 'The Station'. Steve didn't want to go, felt the odd person there, but the other two insisted that he joined them. Veronica wanted to talk future dates to book and took her planner with her. After they ate their meals, they drank Kedy brew and discussed plans.

"I have a date open in three terms and another one in seven," Veronica said looking at her planner.

"That works for me." Steve replied while looking at his ledger, "Give me the dates and I'll get a cash advance to you tomorrow."

"Steve," she said calmly, "you don't have to worry about paying in advance; we only do that to first time bookings."

"Great," he said as he started copying down the dates from her files.

Veronica turned to her left and looked at Hawk leaning back in his chair with a content look on his face. "That Fana bird egg was delicious," he said, "It filled me up."

"I can't remember the last time that I had a meal so good," Veronica added.

"I'm surprised!" Hawk announced. "With you being such a high demand band, I'd expect you'd eat like the best that's offered."

"Once in a while, yes," Veronica stated, "but when you've got to pack up and leave to the next place in a hurry, you only get time for slop food and of course, most of it tastes like shit."

"Then I'd love to catch up everything you missed." Hawk suggested.

Veronica turned to Hawk and smiled. All this time during their business talk, she had her left hand on his right knee under the table. After Steve was done with recording the information, he shut his book and looked at Veronica. "I want to thank you again for taking on Little Chicago. Thank your band for me."

"It was my pleasure," Veronica stated.

"So, with that," Steve said standing up, "I bid both of you good night."

"Good night." They both repeated.

As they watched Steve walk out of the restaurant, Veronica turned toward Hawk and wrapped her arms around him his shoulders, "Now, how about starting your tour?"

"Where do you want to start?"

"How about your place?" she whispered in his ear.

****

Just outside of Serin Base's boarder, a large war vessel separated into three smaller ships and they went on different designated paths. The center ship was the largest and the two side ships were identical but still carried very heavy firepower. They all would reach their destination within the next course and wait for their orders to be carried out.

CHAPTER 10

The large tanker that was fastened to the bottom of Sheila looked awkward and bulky. From the ground, Sheila could hardly be seen, only her wings protruding over the sides. Even though there were doubts that she could carry it from the ground crew, she could easily carry twice the weight. Attaching the tanker was the difficult part because Sheila was so small. In a normal hookup system, it would only take six chain rods to connect the tank, but Sheila needed sixteen. Her circular head is what caused all the trouble. The hook up took fifteen taps longer to get ready. They were already behind.

Katrina and Jason held on to each other on the landing area in front of Sheila. This would be the longest time they would be apart from each other.

"I'm going to miss you," Katrina said kissing his cheek.

"Aw, you'll be buried in so much of your inventory that the time will fly by and I'll be back before you know it." Jason said looking deep into her eyes. "I'm going to miss you very much as well."

Hum* "Hurry up down there, damn it; I want to get this thing off my ass as soon as possible!"

"Coming mother," Jason yelled. Then he planted a long kiss on Katrina's lips. The touch warmed him up inside, and they started to caress each other's backs. Longer and longer the kiss went on, making their hearts beat faster and faster. She started to moan with pleasure as he….

Hum* "HURRY UP!"

"Alright, alright, I'm coming," Jason yelled as he let Katrina go.

Katrina watched him as he entered a lifter and it took him up to Sheila's entrance door. Once he stepped off the lift, she could no longer see him. Within a couple of ticks, Sheila slowly pulled up and off the area and was heading toward the sky.

****

After leaving 'The Station', Veronica and Hawk walked all over the port. He pointed out the good spots as well as the bad, which included the hotel she was staying in. She ran into her room, gathered her things and cancelled her reservation. Hawk graciously paid for the late cancellation fee.

They soon found themselves at the Grand Gate and at the door to Jason's room. When he opened the door and stepped in, Veronica's response was unexpected.

"Holy shit!" Veronica yelled, "If only I could stay in rooms like this when I traveled!" She walked in, looked around the room and threw her bag of belongings on the floor.

Hawk glanced around himself, taking in the rooms' amenities, "He told me that he has been in this room for about ten rotations now, he...."

Veronica grabbed him and pulled him toward her. She embraced him in a hard kiss, putting her tongue into his mouth. She started moaning as she grabbed his jacket and yanked it down off his shoulders. He pulled off her red coat that she wore. Both jackets fell to the floor. Then with one swift jerk, she ripped open his shirt and the buttons bounced all over the room. He grabbed onto her blouse and ripped it in half exposing her bare chest and she pulled her arms out of the sleeves and threw it to the floor as well. She immediately knelt down and started unbuckling his pants as he ran his fingers through her thick red hair. Once undone, she pulled his pants and underwear down to his ankles and he stepped out of them. She stood up again and pulled off her pants and panties and aggressively threw them down on the floor.

She grabbed him and backed him up to the couch and forced him to sit down. She leaned forward for a kiss and roughly bit his lip. He jumped but gave into the pain sensation. His heart started pounding as she stuck her tongue into his mouth again and swirled it around.

Then a sudden sizzling noise caught her attention, and she let her kiss go and looked into his eyes.

They started to turn bright green.

"Oh my god, your eyes, they..." she said in shock.

"I know," he said, pulling her down for another strong kiss.

That's when Veronica really started going wild. She first started lightly biting his lips again, and then worked down his cheek onto his neck. She bit him again there and then worked down to his right shoulder where she really clamped down on his flesh. He started to lightly bleed. Then she worked herself farther down toward his right nipple where she sucked it, then bit it hard. He let out an exhilarating sigh and then put his hands on her shoulders. She then went further down toward his stomach and noticed that he had no belly button. She shrugged off her thoughts and then continued her down ward approach toward his lap. She slowly put him into her mouth. He stretched his legs out in excitement as she gently took him in and then back out. The sensation was making him shiver in pure adrenalin and he closed his eyes and tilted his head back. More and more she took him as she ran her hands all over his chest. Then, suddenly, she pulled herself up and shoved him back on the couch on his back. She then climbed up on top of him and inserted him deep within her. She folded her legs out to his sides and raised herself up and down upon him.

She bounced several times making her breasts jiggle uncontrollably. He reached his arms around her back and pulled her left breast into his mouth. He bit down hard on her nipple and she let out a cry of excitement. He started sucking hard on her breast and left a blood mark on her skin. She continued her motions and leaned her head back.

"OH GOD! Fuck me, you animal, FUCK ME!" she yelled.

She grabbed the back of his head and she flipped them over onto the floor next to the couch without him leaving her from within. With her now on the bottom and him on top, he moved in and out on her slowly and gently. She took her nails and dug them into his back. The scratches where long and deep and made him even more aroused. She screamed again.

"Harder," she yelled, "HARDER!"

He complied with her request and became even more aggressive with his actions. She arched her back and screamed louder and louder as she became frantic.

"YES! YES! YES, HOLY SHIT!" She yelled again as she threw her arms out to her sides.

Her left hand found the couch cushion, and she started squeezing it with all her energy. Her body felt like it was filling with intense heat as her mind totally went hysterical as she burst into one of the strongest orgasms she had ever had. Shivers went down her legs and they trembled as she reached her arms around him again and dug her fingers deeper into his back.

He started to reach his peak and propped himself up on his hands and let out a long yell. Every muscle in his body tensed as he had his orgasm.

With a last gasp, he fell down on top of her, and they both didn't move for a while. The sweat covering their bodies made sucking sounds between their bellies and it made Veronica laugh.

She looked deep into his bright green eyes and brushed his hair gently with her right hand.

"Please," she said between breaths, "Don't let this become a one-night stand."

"Not a chance," he answered pulling her head up and grabbing another kiss.

And then they started again.

****

A knock at the front window broke Steve's concentration from counting last night's sales. He walked over toward the front door, glasses already on and unbolted the lock. He opened it up to see Katrina standing outside.

"Well, good morning young lady, what brings you here?"

"You said you would bend my ear," she said as she held up two large bags, "I brought breakfast."

"Never turn down a woman with food," he said as he let her inside. They walked over to the bar, and she set the bags on the top counter. Steve grabbed utensils, napkins and two glasses of Berkley juice. After they set up their settings, they both sat down.

"I hope you like grapie egg rolls." She stated, opening a bag.

"Love them," he said, "so, where do you want to start?"

"Let me start first with this," Katrina said pulling a book out of the other bag. "This is how I found out about Earth." She laid the book on the counter, and Steve's eyes widened.

"How in the world did this, where did......" he said as he picked up the book

"Jason said the same thing." She said laughing,

"What is it you want to know; I mean about Earth?"

"Jason said that it blew up, what happened?" she said as she pulled the rolls out of the bag and gave one to Steve.

Steve sighed, "I happened. Well, so to speak. I was in the military," he stated as he pulled a chain up from his shirt containing dog tags, "and I was assigned to drop a bomb that was supposed to end the war, but instead, it ended the planet."

"Jason has the same thing on his neck, what are they?"

"These are called dog tags. It's shows identification about the person who wears them. We both still wear them to remind us of our fallen comrades. Neither of us like talking about it, we lost families as well."

"Were you married?"

"Yes, a wife and three kids," he sighed.

"I'm sorry that I brought it up." She said putting her hand on his shoulder. "What about Jason, was he married too?"

"No, he was just a young fancy-free kid then. He did have a lot of relatives in Illinois though."

"From what he told me; Sheila was the one that saved you."

"That, I'm very thankful for. She maybe a pain in the ass at times, but she has the most advanced system I ever seen." He took a bite of the roll and sauce dribbled down his cheek. Grabbing his napkin, he wiped off the mess.

"I know that there were three of you, what happened to the other guy?"

"Oh, Rodger," Steve said between bites, "he's no longer with us. He was a hot head and always wanted things done his way. I'm glad to see him go."

Katrina took a bite from her roll and then wiped her mouth. "I really don't want to come across like I'm being nosey, but..."

"Naw, don't worry about it. I'm enjoying this conversation. In fact, I wanted to get to know you better because Jason has really taken a shine to you. I'm kind of like a father figure to him. I feel that I need to meet the possible future Mrs. Powell."

Katrina blushed, "Don't you think you're being hasty?"

"Do you love him?"

"Yes, very much," she said without hesitation.

"And I know he's very much in love with you, so what's the problem?"

"Jason just seems a little reserved."

"He was hurt in a romance about two years ago, and it hit him pretty hard."

Katrina looked puzzled, "Two what?"

"Sorry, talking Earth time, I mean two rotations ago."

"Well, one can only hope." She smiled.

"You'll be fine," Steve said as he patted her hand and turned to get the juice container behind them.

Katrina smiled, "Thanks. Now what can you tell me about Hawk?"

Steve swallowed the bite in his mouth. Then he refilled the glasses and set the pitcher down. "What I'm about to tell you doesn't leave this room."

Katrina nodded.

"Hawk doesn't like anyone knowing what he is. He came from a laboratory that did experiments on animals. They used a lot of unstable drugs and tested their theories on many things. It's downright inhuman what they did. They have a lot of financial backers, though."

Katrina's eyes saddened, "How awful. Where was he originally born?"

"He wasn't" Steve said while taking a drink of his juice. "He was grown in the lab with a lot of the unstable material they used."

Katrina held her hand to her mouth. The thoughts of the poor boy being grown made her feel selfish. She always thought that she had a bad childhood at the orphanage; it was nothing compared with what he would have gone through. "Is he ill, or diseased?"

"Oh no, nothing like that, the experiment was a success. He became the most advanced experiment they made. Then one day, they discovered their perfect product escaped."

"So, he's on the run?"

"Actually," Steve laughed, "it would be suicide for anyone to try to catch him. You see, every genetic makeup of his body is altered. His speed, his hearing, his brain patterns, hell even his eyes change color depending upon his mood."

"How did you guys meet him?"

"He wandered into the club just before Jason and Rodger got into a pretty bad fight. He's been with us ever since."

"Wow, I'm speechless. And from what I gather, he does a lot of Sheila's repairs."

"Actually, it was Jason that did most of the work in changing Sheila from ZEUS. Hawk is just a techno adviser. Of course, his advanced knowledge could put us all out to pasture."

"Does he have an implanted com chip like Jason has from Sheila?"

"No, Jason is the only one with a locator chip in his skin. Hawks brain wave patterns were too unstable for Sheila to comprehend."

"Last question," she said taking the last bite of her roll, "tell me about Sheila."

"Oh great, saving the hardest for last, huh?' he smiled, "I'll start from when we found Tego…."

****

This time their sexual experience ended on the kitchen floor. The berries and cream from the refrigerator added another level to the experience. Veronica's mind was so overwhelmed with satisfaction she could barely breathe. They both sat on the floor, nude, as the heat from their bodies rose around them.

"God, I think I lost twenty pounds." Veronica said exhaustedly.

"Want to lose some more?" Hawk said

"Are you kidding me?" she said falling back on her back, her breasts wiggling as she wiped sweat from her forehead.

Hawk leaned over to her and licked her left breast. "No, I'm not kidding. Let's try the bathroom this time."

"But don't you need to, you know, reload? Don't guys have to recharge?"

"You mean orgasms? I can have endless ones. I'm not restricted in that department," he said batting his eyes.

"You really do soar above the rest, don't you?"

He licked her breast again. "Lets' go," and he jumped up and walked out of the kitchen.

She slowly pulled herself up, having no energy to move and got herself to stand with the support of the counter. She reached over and took several gulps of water from a plastic bottle that sat on top. "I need to rest," she said with a large sigh.

"You can just lie flat, I'll do all the work," he said laughing, "Come on"

She got a real annoyed look on her face, "Just lie flat? Oh, that sounds really fucking passionate." She picked up a rounded fruit off the counter, "I ought to throw this azuka fruit at you."

"Go ahead and try," he said egging her on. She threw it and he caught it in midair with his left hand. Her surprised look on her face made her speechless.

"Is that the best you can do?"

"I'll just come over there and beat the shit out of you," she said raising a fist in the air.

"Go ahead and try," he repeated.

She ran toward him and tackled him to the ground.

And then they started again.

****

Katrina had all her notes from her home records and was in the elevator in the tower. She was going to drop off all that she had done to Careese and Kyler in case she didn't get back.   When the door opened, she walked to her office to find both of her assistants standing in there already.

"What are you doing here," Careese yelled, "You're supposed to take the day off."

"I will carry you out," Kyler added.

"Relax you two," Katrina said laying all the papers on the desk. "I'm just dropping off everything I had at home so you can finish it. I talked to Tower support, and I'm taking a vacation for a week."

Careese held out her hands like she was going to faint, "Hold me up, Kyler, I think I'm going to pass out. Did you say vacation?"

"Yes, and I'm counting on you two to have a perfect inventory count. This has got to be right for the start of the fiscal cycle."

"I didn't hear a word you said after vacation." Kyler added, "I'm still trying to comprehend that word."

"Me too," Careese said as she sat down in a chair.

"Funny, you two are very funny. I knew there was a reason I kept you guys around." Katrina turned to Careese, "there is something I need from you, though."

"What?"

"I'd love to have you over for dinner tomorrow night to meet Jason."

"I'd love to, that is if we get all of this done," she said slamming her hand on the pile of papers.

"I'll call you when it's time, ok?"

"Great." Careese smiled.

"How come nobody asks me for dinner?" Kyler sniffled.

"Because you have a jealous wife who would have all our heads on a platter, that's why." Careese acknowledged.

"Good bye, guys," waved Katrina as she left the office.

CHAPTER 11

Green meadows surrounded the area as a cool breeze blew his hair. Birds were singing and he could smell the aroma of nearby flowers. He was lying on his back and seeing objects in the clouds above him. He saw a rabbit, a boat and even a football. He heard a voice behind him and he turned to see Katrina dressed in a wedding gown. She held up her arms and waved him forward. He stood, walked toward her and held her tight. Her body felt good and warmed him all over. He gazed into her eyes and leaned forward for the kiss that....

Hum* "Jason, sleeping beauty, we're approaching Zeta's atmosphere."

Jason jumped out of sleep, "Damn it, Sheila, why did you wake me up now?"

Hum* "If you want to see that dream again, I have it recorded."

"I don't care about what I saw; I wanted to experience what was to happen!"

Hum* "Well, I saved you the trouble. I didn't feel like watching anyway."

"Who said you had to watch?"

No answer.

"If you were only human, you'd understand."

Hum* "If I were human, I'd probably kill myself."

"Do as you please, I'm going to live and enjoy it."

Hum* "Enjoy what?"

"SEX," Jason shouted.

Hum* "Whoopee, stick it in, pull it out, sounds rather boring if you ask me."

"It's all in the ...the...ah hell forget it. You'll never understand. Now radio ground control and let's get this wart off your ass."

Hum* "Love to."

It didn't take long for Jason to find the medical team for the supplies. They were already waiting for him on the landing platform. Getting the tanker off Sheila was easier than putting it on, and she was unclamped within ten minutes. Jason received the rest of his pay and returned to the bedroom in Sheila.

"I'm going out for a while and explore," he said while opening a drawer in a cabinet.

Hum* "Well, you be careful. I hear that Zeta is the pit of the system. Most of the people who live here are all the rough ones."

"That's why I'm taking this," he stated as he pulled out a sheath that had a bowie knife, He bent over and pulled up his right pants leg and attached the strap. "I'm taking no chances."

Hum* "And you better not drink too much, you want to be alert."

"You're not telling me anything I don't know. If you get stinking drunk in this place, you'll probably wind up in a gutter somewhere with no clothes on."

Hum* "Sounds kinky!"

Jason started walking toward the exit door, his hand already resting on his gun. "I won't be out long, just a couple of hours."

Hum* "Ok, and by the way, I'm going to have to shut down for a while."

"What for?"

Hum* "Getting closer to the sun is making my solar panels overheat, I need to cool them off."

"That's strange," Jason said with a quizzical look, "That shouldn't happen. I'll crawl in you when we get back to Largo."

Hum* "After you crawl back into Katrina?"

"Yes, and by the way," he stated harshly, "thanks a lot for making me think that she farted on the bridge the other day!"

Hum* "What are you talking about? I wouldn't.... AH HAWK!"

"Yes Hawk. I'll see you later." Jason stepped outside.

What a lie. As soon as Jason left her, she shut off his communication chip so that he would think she was turned off. Nothing was wrong with her solar panels, she just wanted to come up with a good excuse to become absent for a while. She had never been to this planet and wanted to record as much data that she could get. In fact, with the extra time here, she was planning on investigating the first two planets, Mego and Rage, as well. They were all lined up together and it would be easy for her to input data and be back within a few hours. She slowly lifted off the landing pad and headed toward orbit.

Hum* "Input section three hundred and twenty-three, memory slot fifteen, the Planet Zeta. Zeta is the third planet in the system. It has no government or organization controlling it. Unlike Tego, who has individual owners and their laws, Zeta harbors all the drifters of the system. Population is seven million, six hundred and fifty-three thousand and twenty-two. Most of the inhabitants are smugglers, pirates, and criminals.

Several other creatures inhabit the planet. Most of them are carnivores and many eat human flesh. An underground race known as the Klebits, dig tunnels up to the surface and wait for something to fall to their death. In the skies fly the Hellgars, large winged birds that can carry one hundred and fifty pounds. Most of the time, they flock alone, but like sharks on Earth, when one attacks, a feeding frenzy begins.

On a geographical angle, Zeta is six parts land and four parts water. A daily cycle is twenty-nine earth hours and it makes a yearly rotation every one thousand eight hundred and thirty-nine days. In conclusion, Zeta is dangerous in the air, land and below ground which makes it a very bad pace to be."

Sheila shut off her memory recorder and shot out of Zeta's orbit headed toward the second planet, Mego.

****

The mirror in the bathroom was so steamed up that if anyone wanted to see their reflection, it would have to be cleaned.

The entire room felt like a sauna. Even the clean towels hanging on the rack were damp.

Veronica was in the free-standing tub, still nude, and her hair was completely matted down. Her arms were hanging over the sides and she was barely moving. Her face looked overheated and completely drenched in sweat. Hawk sat on the floor, gently caressing her right leg which also dangled out of the tub.

"Feeling good?" Hawk said gently.

"I can't feel my legs," she said with a very tired voice, "I think you paralyzed me,"

"What's next?" Hawk asked enthusiastically.

"Well," she panted, "we've been up all night and I'm either in need of some sleep or something to eat. If I try eating first, I'll fall asleep in the food, so I vote that we get some rest."

"I'll tell you what," Hawk said wrapping his arm around her leg and putting his head on top, "You take a nap, and I'll go get us something to eat."

"What?" she said exhaustedly lifting her head, "Don't you need to get some sleep as well?"

Hawk stood up and grabbed a glass at the sink and filled it with water. He handed it to her and she gulped it down. "I don't sleep." He casually stated.

"How the hell, what do you... What are you anyway, some sort of machine?"

"Get some sleep. I've got a couple of errands to do, and I'll be back in about three courses with some food." He started heading to the door, "Then while we eat, I'll tell you everything you need to know, Roni"

She smiled at him. "The only person who ever called me Roni was my father."

"I'm sorry," he replied, "didn't mean to intrude on that memory."

"No," she stated, "it's ok. In fact, I like hearing it from you."

"Then get some rest, Roni, and I'll be back in a couple of courses."

She gathered what energy she could to smile at him as he left the room. She started to try to get up to go lay in the bed, but changed her mind and fell asleep in the tub.

****

So far, Jason had managed to stay out of trouble. Just the sight of his seven sixteen pistols made several people back away. He had been to three bars, the last one being a strip club. It also proved to be the rowdiest. Lots of fights filled the bar and how anyone managed to enjoy living here was beyond his comprehension. It all came down to who you knew, what your needs were and your freedom. Since there were no governing rules, people were free to do whatever they pleased. That would explain the overall inhabitants of the planet.

In the last ten minutes, one man picked up a bottle and busted it over another man's head. The unconscious body laid on the floor for only a couple of seconds before several other people stripped him clean of his belongings.

Jason finished his drink quickly and decided to call it a night. He got up from the table and walked to the front door, cautiously walking between people. When he stepped outside, he could smell an odor of rotting food. His curiosity was satisfied when he saw the overflowing garbage bin on the side of the building. Several rat-like creatures were scurrying around its spilled contents.

As he rounded the corner, he turned into two large men waiting for him. His hand reacted and reached for his pistol, but one of the men grabbed his hand.

"No, no, no," said one of the men in a raspy voice, "we mustn't be a hero."

He grabbed Jason by the shoulders and dragged him over to the wall next to the garbage bin. The other man followed and pulled Jason's pistol out of its holster.

"These babies aren't cheap," said the other man through his rotted teeth. "This guy has rolets."

"Give us your rolets and we'll spare you," the first man said slamming Jason up against the wall. The impact of the hit made Jason's dog tags fly out from under his shirt.

"Eh, what's this?" said the man holding Jason's gun as he yanked the chain off Jason's neck.

That was it. Jason swung his foot as hard as he could and kicked the man holding him in the balls. The man yelled and grabbed his crotch doubling over. Jason then charged the other man holding his belongings. They struggled and fought as both maintained their grip on the gun. When they backed into the garbage bin, Jason almost had his weapon free when he started hearing a snapping sound beneath his feet.

Suddenly, the ground under them fell away and they found themselves plummeting down a deep hole. The last thing Jason remembered was the darkness and hitting the bottom.

****

Hum* "Input section three hundred and twenty-four, memory slot fifteen, the planet Mego."

Sheila shot down further into its atmosphere to get better readings. She passed through the red air and leveled out with the ground below, about one mile above it. Steam rose uncontrollably from its surface. A combination of rock and gases made it a very unstable planet.

Hum* "The planet consists of no liquid whatsoever for most of the planet is too hot to sustain it. Volcanic activity is strong but when the planet spins on the cool side, the lava becomes solidified. It takes fifteen Earth days for it to make one revolution. Being such a small celestial body, the size of what used to be Earth's moon; doesn't really classify it as a planet. Although the data shows that it does revolve around the system's sun, meaning it has an orbit. It has no life forms and looks to be a planet being born."

She leveled herself above a large volcano that was not active and lowered down inside.

Hum* "I'm descending into an inactive volcano and judging by the rock formations has been for some time. The air temperature in the crater is seven hundred and forty-three degrees."

She then raised herself back out and started heading out of the planet's obit.

Hum* "In all conclusion, Mego is a child, a planet in developing stages. It will be quite some time before it's ready to hold life, if ever."

Her memory tapes clicked off as she banked herself toward the left and toward a small red dot in front of her. That dot was the planet Rage.

****

Hawk walked into Little Chicago, with his Trill on his shoulder, and was instantly approached by Steve.

"I see you have another trill, are you going to lose this one too?"

"No, I'm kind of fond of this guy." Hawk said reaching up and scratching its neck. It started to purr to his touch.

"I need a favor from you," Steve said pleadingly. "Last night was so busy that I gave half the crew the night off tonight. I could use some help running things. Katrina's going to be here any minute and help with waiting on tables. I still need another bartender and a bouncer. Can you help?"

Hawk sat down at one of the barstools, "Only if you let me keep the Trill in the back wine cellar. I don't want to leave him at Jason's hotel room. The cleaning staff has a real mess to clean up as it is."

"Mess," Steve said sitting on the stool next to him, "What did you do?"

"Well," Hawk coyly smiled, "I've been with Veronica all night and we, well, I mean..."

"Good God, man, you didn't kill her, did ya?"

"Of course not, but she's probably pretty dehydrated. We..."

"No," Steve held up his hand to stop him, "I don't want to know. It's none of my business."

"Let's just say she's sleeping right now, and I'm getting ready to pick up lunch."

"Very thoughtful of you, young man," Steve said nodding his head, "So can you help me?"

"Yes, I'll see if Veronica will help as well. She told me that she used to bar tend for a while."

"Perfect" Steve said slapping him on the back, "So what's the story with you two? This isn't going to turn into a fast fling, is it?"

"I don't think so. She really opened up to me last night when you were closing up the bar. We found we had a lot in common."

"Does she know about you?" Steve said cautiously.

"I'm telling her when I go back with lunch. I hope it doesn't scare her away. I really love this girl."

"You can never go wrong with the truth. If she loves you for what you are, then it's meant to be. Nobody needs to be false for someone else to like them, nobody. I hope it works out for you."

"Thanks," Hawk said getting up off the stool and walking toward the back room. "I'll put some food and water in there for him, and then I'll be back in a course."

"If he shits on the floor, you're cleaning it up!"

****

Katrina walked into Little Chicago taking off her coat and laying it on a barstool. She was dressed in a pair of dark blue slacks and a maroon blouse. Even though the door was unlocked, there was nobody in the club yet. She didn't even see Steve.

"Hello? Is anyone in here?"

Steve stepped out of the back room, "Over here, little lady, we're all back here getting stock to fill the bar."

Katrina walked to the back storage area and met the other five people that would be working with her tonight. She was a little shy at first, but with the other's instructions; she started getting more and more comfortable. Aiden started showing her how easy it was to take orders and where to pick them up. She also showed her a diagram chart of the floor seating and what section she would be working. Katrina was actually getting very excited about the whole idea. It was a different pace from the office and made her feel adventurous.

Ten taps later, they were all gathered at the bar, looking at the assortment of bottles across the counter top, and Steve was counting the tallies.

"I need just a couple of Fireball mixes from the cellar and we'll be ready."

"I'll get it," Katrina said anxiously and trotted off toward the back.

The front door opened up and several of tonight's dancers walked in taking their coats off and heading toward the stage door when a loud scream came from the back room accompanied by breaking glass. Everyone was startled.

"Oh, shit," Steve uttered, "I forgot about that damn Trill."

Katrina walked out, backwards, pointing toward the back room. "There's an animal in the cellar, it growled and jumped at me!"

"You didn't get bit, did you?" Steve said with concern as he rushed toward her.

"No, but I slammed the door before it had a chance to get out," she said sitting on a stool to catch her breath.

"That's Hawks' pet, I'll have him explain it to you when he gets here."

Katrina took a drink of water handed to her by Aiden.

"Welcome to Little Chicago," Aiden said with a smile.

****

When Hawk returned to Jason's hotel room, he found that Veronica had taken a shower and was now dressed in a tank top with slacks and sitting on the couch. She smiled at him as he brought food over to the table in front of her.

"Well rested, Roni?" he said pulling the containers out of the bags.

"Yes, and now I'm famished. What did you bring?"

"Guna steak and capa beans."

Veronica made a groan of excitement and opened up the box in front of her. Hawk sat next to her and opened up his box as well. Then, Veronica paused in deep thought. She turned to Hawk and held his hand.

"Hawk, darling, I need to tell you something."

She had his attention fully. Whatever it was, he could see that it was serious in her eyes. "Tell me anything you wish, it's safe with me."

She swallowed hard. "I can't describe what I'm feeling about you right now. All my life I've always been on the run; not from someone chasing me, but from life catching me. I was in a very serious relationship once and I opened myself up to this guy. He really meant a lot to me. I have a habit of being very forward and most people can't handle that." She took another bite of her food and when she swallowed, she continued. "When I tried to express my inner feelings, he got scared and, well, left me. I used to think it was my brashness that scared him away but I learned to accept that I was just too much to handle. Maybe it's the way I present myself or the way I am during sex. Whatever it is, I've accepted that I was some sort of freak."

Hawk's reaction to that word got him to lift up his head in alertness.

"I thought love was just a fantasy world that would never be for me. I had given up cycles ago."

"Sounds like someone else I know," Hawk said thinking about Jason.

"But, Hawk, you've shown me that someone can love me for who I am. You've been able to handle everything about me."

"Someone recently told me that you can never go wrong with the truth. If you love someone for what they are, then it's meant to be. Nobody needs to be false for someone else to like them," Hawk smiled, "nobody."

Veronica smiled and took another bite. "But do you find me too hard to handle, possibly crazy?"

"Not a chance," Hawk answered. "People always have a tendency to run away from what they don't understand. They get frightened because people express their inner feelings or because they can't handle the truth."

A tear ran down Veronica's cheek, and Hawk reached up and wiped it off.

"Veronica, I love you." He said with a smile. "Nothing you can do will make me leave, nothing."

She reached over and kissed him lightly on the right cheek. "That's sweet."

"Now," he said setting down his utensil and turning toward her, "I need to tell you something about me that very few people know and hopefully I won't chase you away."

She tensed up, not knowing what to expect. She took a deep breath and slowly let it out.

"Are you ready?" he asked.

"Whatever it is, I'll understand, for I love you too."

****

Hum* "Input section three hundred and twenty-five, memory slot fifteen, the planet Rage."

Sheila pulled closer to the planet as she started to record more information.

Hum* "The planet is four-fifths molten lava and one fifth rock. The ground is composed of lava pools walled by massive rock formations. Its revolution is equivalent to one hundred and twenty Earth days."

Sheila shot her way down closer through the atmosphere and found it a little hotter than she expected.

Hum* "The temperature of the air is reading around one thousand nine hundred and four, which is the largest reading that I can pick up. I'm now entering the planet side closet to the sun."

She flew herself closer to the planet, all her solar panels turned off. Then, suddenly, something crossed her scanners in disbelief.

Hum* "This is very strange, but I'm picking up life forms on the planet!"

A loud snap came from her back end and her altitude started to fall.

Hum* "OH SHIT," she yelled while trying to regain her control. The flight control system was inoperative and she was going down fast. Before she knew it, she had fallen into the gaseous air and disappeared below.

Hum* "JASON!!!!"

CHAPTER 12

A low distant scream awakened Jason from his sleep. Quivering from the disturbance, his body slowly started to take in his surroundings.

First there was the pain, a persistent pain within his head and lungs. He slowly attempted to lift his head but the pain was too intense, and he stopped trying. Every time he tried to breathe; a stabbing pain was produced.

Second, to his senses, was an unbalanced crackling noise that was near to him. Each pop varied in tone and length giving him unlimited possibilities. A stove, chewing gum, a fire, dry spaghetti being split and walking on dry twigs all came to mind.

Third was a warm breeze or current which covered him. The heat stung his cheeks and his body felt overheated.

Next was an odor that smelled like wet musty clothes. It stung the inside of his nose every time he took a breath.

Then, slowly, he opened his eyes.

The small camp fire in front of him danced its shadows off the rocky ceiling above. Each of its sparks crackling different directions gave a hypnotizing effect. Just above the fire hung a large stewing pot, bubbling with some sort of sauce. The steam climbed from the open pot and dissipated in the air above. Jason was covered in a blanket, and leaning up in the corner of what looked like a small cave opening.

Then he noticed a figure on the other side of the fire. It was an older man, maybe in his fifties, with a scraggly beard, and he started edging toward Jason on his knees while holding a large cup.

"Have a swig of stew, lad?" he said holding the cup toward him.

Jason looked skeptically at the glass. The old man lifted the cup and took a drink, then tried to hand it to Jason again. Jason took it in confidence.

"Careful, ot stuff it is," the old man said, "but it'll warm up yer innards enough. Make you feel better."

Jason took a sip of the liquid, its foul stench curling his nose. The stuff tasted bad, but did warm him up on the way down. Its strong smell cleared his nostrils instantly. Looking deeper at the man he could see that he was dressed in ragged clothes, unshaven, scarred all over his face and very dirty.

The old man smiled, his yellow decaying teeth still intact, and jutted out his hand again. "Meat stick?"

Jason slowly reached up and accepted the offer. He sniffed its odd odor before biting it. It reeked, but his stomach was too hungry to be finicky. When he bit down on the coarse thick meat, his pain in his head was intensified and it made him cringe.

"Still urtin?" the old man said, "You've been out for a while." He bit down on his stick and ripped off a chunk.

"Who are you?" Jason asked while pulling off the blanket.

"Name doesn't matt'r, not down ere at least."

"Where's here?" Jason questioned as he glanced around.

"New to tis planet I take it?" the old man asked.

"You mean Zeta, or this hell hole?"

The old man started to cackle, his teeth dully glistening within the fires light. His cackle seemed to rise like a siren, and then drift off. When he stopped, he looked side to side then leaned forward to where his face was just inches away from Jason's. "Tis ell ole, you talk about, is." Then he took another bite of the meat. "Tis is ellgar meat and is te only ting to eat, tat is if yer lucky enough to catch one, but mind ya, you get used to te taste."

"How long you been here?" Jason said taking another sip of the stew.

"Time doesn't matt'r down ere."

Jason rubbed his forehead and felt a large lump.

"Yer lucky you landed on the fat guy when you fell in or your wounds could've been a lot worse. Nutton very serious at least."

Jason's mind started to clear. He remembered falling down the hole. He could remember…

"Do tis belong to you?" the old man said holding his dog tags.

"Yes," Jason said reaching for it, then had it pulled away from his grasp.

"Never seen tis kinda material," the man said looking it over, "it's not expensive, is it?"

"Rolets don't matter down here either now, does it?" Jason looked at him sternly. The old man laughed and tossed the chain at Jason, who put it in his pocket. Jason noticed that his eyes were adjusting to the light and he could see that they were in a small cavern that had four exits leaving the room.

"Did you find anything else lying around me, perhaps a gun?"

"Now, if tere was a gun, don't cha tink I'd have it? Tat would be a great weppon to have. Make me live a lot easier." The old man looked over Jason's body, "You're gonna need sometin to defend yerself." The man turned and pointed toward the corner, "everytin I find I trow in tat pile, elp yerself.'

"Defend myself from what?" Jason asked.

"The Klebits, man, ow ignorant are you?"

"What the hell is a Klebit?" Jason said slowly standing up.

"Tey be monsters," he instructed him, "tey dig up to te surface and wait for sometin to drop down."

Jason stood up and limped over toward the pile on the floor. He saw a lot of clothing, jewelry, shoes, and a few knifes and sticks. The best thing he saw was a machete.

Then, within the silence, a low growl came from one of the exits.

"Urry," the old man said, "Get a weppon and get by te fire, tey don't like te fire. Tey only hunt in twos so it'll be easy for us to get tem.'

A louder and closer growl sounded again, just in the archway.

The old man was wrong. Three dark brown hairy beasts, running on all fours, ran toward them. Jason reached down and pulled up the machete just in time to use it one of the creature's heads. He couldn't get a clear glance at what they looked like; he only knew that they sounded pissed and hungry. The old man was slashing at the other two when another ran in from the cavern. Jason saw his chance and ran out of the exit to his right. As he ran down the tunnel, he could hear the scream of the old man as it echoed off the cavern walls.

****

Little Chicago was half full when Hawk and Veronica arrived. She went behind the counter and told Steve that she had bartended for about two cycles for a friend of hers on Tego. Steve accepted her offer graciously. He started showing her around the stations behind the bar to get her familiarized with the system.

Katrina and the other waitresses had been working the floor and were keeping things moving. Aiden took the section next to Katrina's just in case she needed help. The place was beginning to fill up due to the dancers starting in the next half course. Aiden noticed that Katrina was doing just fine, so far.

Hawk was leaning up against the bar, next to the pickup station, when Katrina arrived to pick up her order,

"Having fun? "Hawk asked.

"This is exciting! I never knew how fun this would be," she said while she placed the drinks on her tray. "You just type in the order on your data pad and when you get up here, they are ready to go. I thought I was going to have to memorize each table."

"Yep, Steve has the best of everything here." Hawk added.

"Oh, by the way," Katrina said sternly at Hawk, "I ran into your little pet today, and it scared the hell out of me!"

Hawk snickered, "Sorry."

Just then, Aiden rushed up next to Katrina. "Hey, you got a couple of our regulars at table seven that tend to get really rude and raunchy. Do you want me to take them?"

Katrina turned to her, "No, it's ok. I wanted to experience the job, so I might as well get the whole experience." She turned with her full tray and went back out onto the floor.

"She's having too much fun," Aiden said shaking her head.

"Ya, but you've got to admire her spirit," Hawk said.

"Hey," said a harsh woman's voice behind the bar, "Do you get paid to stand around?"

Hawk and Aiden turned to see Veronica behind the bar with Steve standing next to her.

"No ma'am," they both answered.

"Then, let's get busy!" she said with a snap in her voice.

Hawk walked out to mingle in the crowd and Aiden went to her next table. Steve turned to Veronica and smiled.

"I love a bartender with a whip!" Steve chortled.
looked her over from top to bottom and one of them winked at her.

"What can I get you two gentlemen?" she asked.

"Say," said the first guy pulling the cigar out of his mouth, "When do the dancers start taking their clothes off?"

"It's not that kind of a club, sir." She said calmly.

"Well, ain't that the shit," said the winker. "Then I'll have a Laser twenty-two."

The other man holding the cigar said, "I'll take a bottle of Kasdar brew." Then he leaned toward her, "When do you take YOUR clothes off?"

Katrina just ignored them and walked off toward the bar. The two men started to laugh and Aiden at the nearby table leaned over to them.

"Won't you guys ever grow up?" she said as she pointed her finger at them harshly, "BEHAVE!"

They started laughing again.

Katrina this time picked up three tables' orders at the same time. She was feeling very confident in her balancing and left the bar with her orders to go to table seven first. The men taunted her again when she set their drinks down; one even blew a kiss at her. She turned and proceeded to her next table and delivered the drinks to three men who looked to be in their younger twenties. On her way to the third, she walked past table seven again, and one of the men reached out for her.

"Nice ass, sweet cheeks," he yelled as he slapped her in the ass. The surprise attack made her lose her balance and she dropped the remaining drinks on the floor. Glass and liquid shattered and splattered all over the place and she felt embarrassed. She bent over to pick up the glass fragments to put them on the now empty tray and the men started laughing louder, until....

"How about slapping me in the ass and see what happens."
The two men turned to see Hawk standing at the table.
"Run along, little man, we big boys are playing."
Katrina got up and moved away from the area.
"I think it's time for you to leave." Hawk said calmly.
"Yeah, and who's gonna make me, you pee wee?" said the man with the cigar.
"Last chance," Hawk announced.
"GET LOST!" yelled the other man as he threw the Kasdar bottle straight at Hawk's face. Hawk caught the bottle with his right hand, inches in front of his nose.

A loud crash got Steve and Veronica's attention when they saw a chair fly through the air. The other two bouncers ran toward the disturbance, but when they saw who was involved, stood nearby to watch. Several punches were thrown, not one of them by the two men. Just under a matter of ticks, one man laid on the floor on top of the broken table and the other man unconscious in a chair, with his cigar still hanging out of his mouth.

"Can someone help me take this garbage out?" Hawk yelled.
That's when the other bouncers moved in to help him with his request.

****

Although the lava around her bubbled, Sheila could barely sense the area around her. She had landed on one of the rocky formations just to the ledge of one of the lava pools. Her scanners told her that something other than the lava was moving. Her voice system was inoperative and her air compressors were burned out. She couldn't even reach her data storage units. In conclusion, Sheila had amnesia.

Suddenly, something startled her on right side. Some sort of creature sprang out of the lava and onto her hull. She couldn't scan its dimensions for her ability to get an accurate reading was very scrambled. More and more creatures jumped onto her, and she got more confused.

Abruptly, she felt exposed. Her back hatch had opened and something was in her main control shaft. She then lost all systems and became immobilized.

****

He felt like he'd been running for days as he kept turning and twisting among the maze that he was in. The small flashlight that he always carried with him had aided him along, but he knew that it would soon run out of power. The Klebit's roars fell further and further behind him and that eased his nerves. If only he had his gun.

The next tunnel turned him into a larger one, possibly a cave. Many other shafts connected to this one, giving endless ways to get lost. Far ahead at the other end of the tunnel, was light and it looked like sunshine. Jason's pace quickened up and he was nearing to the opening when he heard several growls behind him

"Shit!" he yelled. He heard the word echo over and over again. Then he heard the stampede. The echoes of the running Klebits sounded like an ongoing rumble of thunder. He started running toward the light as several Klebits started coming in through the shafts toward him.

Just as he reached the opening, he lost his footing and fell off a short cliff. When he landed about eight feet below, his heart started to race for he almost slid into a roaring lava stream at the bottom. Still holding the machete in his hands, he stood up and looked around the area. He saw that he was in an open cavern that contained a lava river that flowed toward the right and under a hole in the wall. The heat within was very humid and hot.

Several growls and screams came from above him as he turned and saw four Klebits looking down at him. The light of the lava gave him a clear view of what was chasing him. They had very long fangs and their noses looked like a cross between a dog and an alligator. Their bodies were the size of a grizzly bear and they snapped their jaws and growled but would not come down after him.

Then he noticed the ledge that went over the stream to the other side to his left. Very gently and cautiously he started edging his way over it. All his concentration was on stepping in the right places and not sliding off. When he got about half way across, he noticed the silence. He turned his head and saw that the Klebits were all sitting down with a look of puzzlement on their faces. They kept pitching their heads back and forth like they were trying to hear something. They also kept glancing up as well.

That's when a Hellgar flew down and almost knocked Jason off the ledge. He regained his balance as another one flew down. They looked like bats but at least four times the size. He swung the machete at one and succeeded in cutting off one of its wings. It then fell into the stream below and disintegrated.

More Hellgars flew down as he ran toward the other side trying not to misstep and fall off the ledge. Reaching the end, he leaped for the upper ledge and got a grip on several plant roots hanging out of the dirt. They were very dry and crackled in his hands, but they had strength enough for him to pull himself up and get clear of the area. Several Hellgars filled the air and dove at the Klebits on the other side. They growled and snapped their jaws at the creatures but soon they left the area in defeat.

The bad thing was, in all the rush, he had dropped the machete into the lava below.

****

The neon lights outside of Little Chicago, flashed off as the night came to a close. Inside the staff was cleaning up dirty glasses and tables as the bouncers started sweeping and mopping the floor. All the dancers had already left for the night; the floor show always ends one course before the club closes, and the last customer walked out ten taps ago.

Steve and Veronica were behind the bar, putting up all the refrigerated items and scrubbing down the bar top. Katrina was leaning against the bar cleaning the serving trays.

"This is the last of them, anything else?" she asked.

"No," Steve answered, "You're free to go home, little lady. Thanks again for all your help."

"No problem, I enjoyed this! I'd love to do this again." Katrina said with gusto in her voice.

Veronica leaned over and whispered something in Steve's ear. He nodded a couple of times and then went back to shutting off the registers' power. That's when Hawk came walking out of the back room with his Trill on his shoulder.

"Hey, Roni, look what I have."

Veronica turned from the bar and reacted in delight. She ran up to him but stopped short when the trill hissed at her.

"Don't move fast, you'll spook him." Hawk said as he petted the trill to calm it down. "It will take a while for him to get used to you."

"Hey," yelled Steve from across the bar, "How long are you planning on keeping that thing here?"

"I'll take him to the Hotel tonight; there is a closet that will be perfect as a pet pen." Hawk started walking back to the back, "Until then, I'll keep him in the cellar until we leave."

Veronica sighed, "Isn't it cute?"

"Ya, until it rips your face off," Steve added.

Katrina nodded in agreement as she watched Hawk head toward the back with the creature.

Within a couple of taps, the rest of the employees walked up and told Steve that everything was done. Steve walked them toward the door, unlocked it, let them out, and locked it up again. Everyone had gone home except the four of them; Katrina, Veronica, Hawk and himself.

"Well, get your coat, little lady," he nodded toward Katrina, "I'm walking you home." Steve went behind the bar and grabbed his coat from behind the bar.

"I'll take that offer," she answered as she too grabbed her coat off the employee's coat rack.

Veronica started walking toward the stage steps and turned toward them leaving. "Good night, you two, see you tomorrow, sometime." And she ran up the steps and behind the curtain.

Hawk came out of the back room and saw Steve and Katrina standing by the door. Steve yelled at Hawk across the room, "I'm walking this lady home, do me a favor and lock up for me."

"No problem." Hawk waved.

"Have a good night," Steve said as he opened the door for Katrina and then stepped out. The loud click told Hawk that Steve locked the door from the outside.

That's when the light in the seating area turned off and red lights came on the stage. Loud sassy music started playing as the curtain raised and Veronica, dressed only in lingerie started dancing to the music. A glitter ball started spinning on the ceiling and the music picked up pace. Hawk slowly walked toward the front table and sat down to watch the show. She started dancing seductively around a pole that was attached to the left of the stage. She dipped her head back and swayed her hips back and forth. Spinning herself around the pole, she then lifted herself off the floor upside down. She slowly slid down the pole with her head hanging upside down facing him. When she reached the bottom, she up righted herself and landed her legs into splits. Then she spun around again and pulled herself up the pole into to a standing position. That's when the strip tease began.

Dancing to the rhythm of the music, she took off her top slowly, lightly exposing one breast, then the next. She took the top off, swinging it around her head, and then threw it at her audience. Hawk caught it with his right hand and bit down on it with his teeth. She then spun her back side toward him and then slowly worked down the panties while she bent down in front of him exposing it all. She lifted each leg out slowly, working the red high heels through the holes and then flung the panties at him as well. They landed on the table in front of him. Spinning around again she then landed flat on her back timing it just right with the last beat of the music. Hawk jumped up applauding and ran for the stage.

And then they started again.

****

After numerous shafts, flooded rooms and dead ends, Jason found himself in a large room. A fire was burning in the corner and illuminated everything in the room. Two wooden chairs sat near a table containing an assortment of rubbish. He could smell its foul stench at a distance of ten feet and holding his nose, walked up for a closer look. There on top of the table, laid the remains of a person, at least what was left of it; the head and chest was about picked clean and the legs were barely recognizable.

Gazing around the room, he started looking for anything to use. There was a lot of clothing scattered around, bones and many personal objects. He then noticed a large double-edged sword leaning against the far wall so he walked over and took it. Its blade was razor sharp and he swung it around to test its weight.

Walking over toward the far corner, where he would be able to see both entrances, he sat down with his back up against the wall. Jason let out an exhausting sigh, and started looking at the room around him. Why would Klebits, who ran on all fours, need chairs to sit on and a table to eat off of? Could it be that he found another place that a human survivor lived? Seeing on how everything was so permanent, it couldn't have been because surely the Klebits would have found them by now.

His mind started working on what to do to get out of here. The old man said that they dug tunnels to the surface for prey to fall in, which meant there had to be a lot of tunnels leading up.

His exhaustion took over him and Jason fell asleep.

****

Katrina had already changed into her nightgown and was sitting in her bed reading a book. She was having a hard time trying to concentrate on the words so she put the book down in her lap and glanced around the room. She felt like something was out of place. She's been living in this apartment for almost four cycles now and tonight it seemed different. The emptiness of not having Jason here made the room dull and lifeless. She didn't feel comfortable in this room alone any more.

She picked up the book, put it on her night stand and turned off the light. Jason would be home tomorrow evening and she'll make dinner for him and Careese. She was very anxious for her to meet him. The faster she could get to sleep; the faster tomorrow would come.

****

Everyone was set for the night.

CHAPTER 13

Katrina woke up early, took a shower and went to The Harvester for food. When she stepped in the door, Emmatt greeted her with a hug.

"How's my child doing?" she said, kissing her on the cheek. "How did it go the other night?"

Katrina blushed, thinking about how well it went. "It was fine."

"Fine? FINE?" she exclaimed, "Do you know how ignorant the word fine is?" Emmatt said pointing at one of the chairs for her to sit down in.

Katrina sat down, ready for a lesson from her favorite teacher.

"The word is used for everything. You could have had one of the worst days of your life, and when someone passes you and says, 'How you doing?' the answer is FINE!"

Emmatt started shaking her head and sat down in the chair next to Katrina. "You could have had one of the best times in your life and your answer still would have been 'Fine."

Katrina started to laugh, "You always have a way with bringing things to light, don't you?"

"So, how did it go?" she said putting her hand on her knee.

"I'm in love."

"I knew it, I saw the glow in your face when you walked in," she said clapping her hands.

"I'll tell you all about it while you help me pick something for a special dinner tonight. How's the Glema fish today?"

"Fine," Emmatt said with a laugh.

****

A low growl awoke Jason from his sleep. The sword was still gripped within his hands and he painfully stood to his feet. The growl grew louder and was coming out of the tunnel to the right, so he backed up against the rocky shadows to the left.

Slowly a large Klebit walked in carrying the body of the old man. This Klebit was huge; it was at least eight feet tall and walking on its hind legs. When it walked up to the table, it threw the old man's body on top of the other remains. This Klebits' arms were very muscular, unlike the smaller ones he had encountered, and it grabbed and tore the arm out of the socket of the man's lifeless body. A gushing ripping noise accompanied his grunts as he sat down and started taking bites out of the arm. Saliva dripped from its jaws as it gnawed its way through flesh and bone.

Jason slowly moved toward the exit on the right, sword raised, in hopes that it wouldn't see him. His eyes were pinned on the monster until something shiny caught his eye to the left of the table; it was his seven sixteen pistols. The relief he felt was gratifying but how was he going to reach it? He quickly changed his direction, stepping toward the left and lightly kicked a rock.

The monster suddenly stopped chewing and froze. It cocked its head to the side to concentrate on what noise it just heard. Jason too, froze as sweat ran down his forehead and into his eyes, stinging them. The monster turned its head and saw Jason standing at the far corner.

It stood up and roared, dropping the half-eaten arm on the floor. Jason lunged toward the left side of the beast but was quickly cut off. He swung the sword, forcing it to back off, and tried to get it to move toward the right. It growled again and shuffled itself toward the other side of the room, where Jason originally started. Out of the corner of his eye, Jason could see the gun but if he jumped for it, the creature would have him. Slowly he shuffled his feet closer toward his destination and he tripped on the half-eaten arm.

The monster charged as Jason fell to the ground. He struck the sword into its right shoulder at the same time its vicious left claw hit him on his right side. Both he and the sword were flung into the table knocking it over. Dazed, Jason started scrambling to find the lost sword under all the debris, for he was under the over turned table and had lost his bearings. Sifting through the rubble, he found his pistol. He heard the onrushing Klebit digging through the pile to find him so he rolled onto his back holding the gun at a ready position.

When the table was thrown off of Jason, he was faced with the large beast; arms open wide, blood pouring from its right shoulder and a large roar. The Klebit was faced with the end of a seven sixteen. Jason fired several shots at the head of the beast. He held down the trigger as shot after shot pounded the monster back until it fell to the ground dead on the other side of the room.

Jason dropped his arms in exhaustion. His right side was bleeding from the wound of the Klebit's strike and his sore ribs from the earlier fall made it hard to breathe. He used one of the chairs to regain his balance and exited out the side that the Klebit entered.

****

Sheila was no longer confused, she was fascinated. The small creatures which roamed around her were the most intelligent beings she ever encountered. They were called the Dextronians and they had learned Sheila's system within two hours and twenty minutes. They had found the problems within her and corrected them. Being able to see again, she scanned every detail of their bodies.

The Dextronians had very complicated minds. They had four times the intelligence of her, which was by far more than any mere man. Their bodies, a thick shell-like skin, enabled them to move freely within the lava. They ranged anywhere from three to seven feet and looked similar to a lizard. They had four legs; each with three fingered hands and on the end of each finger was a large claw which gave them the ability to climb the rocky formations. They were not oxygen breathing creatures, for they had no lung support system of any kind. They also contained no digestive system. How they lived, the solution was simple. They had small pores which took impurities out of the lava and into their bodies. Their life span ranged up to one hundred and twenty years and during their lifetime they grew more knowledgeable. When one would die, its brain patterns would be passed to its off spring, making them more advanced. They only mated once in a lifetime and one litter of children would average a number of six offspring.

The odd thing that struck Sheila was that they had no eyes. They saw and gathered information by telepathic impulses, for it was their only language.

In return for repairing her, the Dextronians gained more knowledge from all the data Sheila contained. They now knew of the other planets in the system as well as the planets in Earths system and their history.

Sheila was beyond her normal state. The Dextronians fixed everything in her and even made it more efficient. They went as far as hooking up the particle transfer unit that Hawk was having so much trouble with. She felt completed and ready to go but the Dextronians told her that she was not ready to leave. Something more needed to be done and within the next hour, the Dextronians designed her systems to understand and feel emotions.

At first Sheila was very puzzled by the input, for she didn't understand what was happening. Love, laughter, hatred, and sorrow all flooded into her circuits and then she started experiencing fear, thinking that she would never see Jason again. She started to actually cry, bringing on a sense of selflessness and pity. Then she thought about all the tricks she pulled throughout the years, and it hit her on how cruel they truly were.

The Dextronians calmed her down. They talked to her telepathically through her system and told her she was ready to leave. Her visit was indeed a blessing to them and they gained massive knowledge from the experience. Their reward was to give her the most precious thing to life and to experience the joy it brings.

Sheila was thrilled and thankful at the same time. She bid them farewell and lifted herself off the rocks and out of the planet's orbit. Her love for the Dextronians warmed up her circuits and she understood the meaning. She had to get back to Zeta, pick up Jason and take him home to his love, Katrina.

****

It wasn't far down the corridor that Jason found light. He was standing at the bottom of one of the tunnels that led to the surface. Water cascaded down the sides and trickled further down into cracks on the floor. The air smelled crisp, and he took a deep breath. Several rock formations were sticking out from the walls, and he could see clouds about fifty feet up.

It was a way out. He tossed back his head and let the water splatter on his face. He didn't know where it could have been coming from or what it consisted of, but it felt refreshing. He took a firm grip on the first rock and pulled himself up. The rocks felt strong within the wall and he found it easy to climb. His momentum speeded up as the surface got closer and closer within his reach.

That's when the tentacle grabbed his left leg.

At first, he thought he had snagged onto a tree root, but when it started to tug on him, he panicked. Another tentacle grabbed his right arm and pulled him off the wall's surface. He was hanging in midair when two other tentacles pulled him sideways. He adjusted his vision to see what had had him.

In the wall was a large oval mouth with several teeth. The mouth was at least three feet in diameter and looked like it was all muscle. Its sucking noises mixed with the water trickling over it reminded Jason of the sound when you empty a glass with a straw. He saw two yellow eyes glaring at him from the sides of the mouth and they kept looking around the area. Surrounding the mouth were at least ten tentacles, all wiggling and thrashing around.

Jason struggled to reach his blaster but he couldn't grab it from the holster. The tentacle had a firm grip on his right arm and he couldn't free it. Reaching around his back with his left arm, he successfully got a grip on the handle but then didn't have enough pull to get it out. There was only one thing to do and hopefully he wouldn't shoot himself in the foot doing it.

He pulled the trigger while it was still in the holster. Several shots fired at the creature and one of them managed to shoot out the right eye. The tentacles went into convulsions as Jason fell out of its grip and down toward the bottom again. Quickly thinking, he grabbed one of the tentacles and held on tight. The tentacles continued to thrash about until minutes later; the creature stopped wiggling and was dead. Jason paused and let out a large sigh of exhaustion, then finished his climb to the surface.

Reaching the top, he saw that the hole exited next to a stream that ran just outside the main gate to the landing field. Painfully climbing the fence, he managed to have enough energy to get back to the landing field and to their hanger bay. When he opened the door and found it empty, he was too tired to scream in frustration. Closing the door back up, he crawled over to a corner and fell asleep.

****

The door opening and a low humming within the hanger awoke Jason from his sleep. Opening his eyes, he saw Sheila slowly moving into the building. Groaning as he stood up, he walked over to her hull having just enough energy to get to her back side. "Sheila…" he whispered as he fainted to exhaustion to the floor.

Hum* "OH MY GOD! What have I done?" She yelled as the tone in her speaker sounded like she was going to cry. "Hold on, honey, I'll get you on board and fixed up!'

And within an instant, she transferred him to the bed inside.

****

The orders they had been waiting for finally arrived. All the transmissions had been sent out to commence procedure immediately. The years of planning, gathering equipment, and gathering followers have now come down to this day. Several individuals, all with their own assignment, left their safe houses and started to engage the targets.

CHAPTER 14

Sheila had everything in control. She had scanned Jason and found he had two cracked ribs, several lacerations including a large gash on his right side, and several scrapes and bruises. She used everything she could to get him healthier and by the time they reached Largo, he was walking around the bridge. He had cleaned his wounds himself and applied healing lotion on the cuts. He had also taken several pain pills but the most refreshing help was the six glasses of water.

Sheila had told him everything that happened. Informed him about the repairs and how sorry she was for all the things she'd done to him. First, he thought she was playing another trick on him but when she started to cry, it opened his eyes.

Jason was stunned and he couldn't believe his ears. Sheila's voice even sounded different; softer, fresher, and even compassionate. When she started talking about her love toward him, she even sounded sexier. This was going to take some time for him to adjust to.

Sheila then informed him that they would be in hanger thirty-seven in the next ten minutes and Katrina was already waiting there for him. She had called her and told Katrina what had happened to Jason. She told her not to worry, that he was fine, but to meet them at the hanger when they arrived.

Jason again couldn't believe his ears.

****

Katrina stood waiting for Sheila to arrive at hanger thirty-seven. She had a heavier coat on and had her arms folded around her tightly to keep warm from the breeze. In her left hand, she held a large shopping bag.

Sheila had told her that Jason ran into some trouble on Zeta and got wounded. She said he was ok but needed her to pick up some items from the store to help him heal. She had just enough time to get the items and get here for their arrival.

She turned to see Sheila slowly moving down the strip but something looked odd. Sheila's hull was slightly glowing and it looked like the entire shell was reflective. The glow of her hull made her look brighter and even happier. Katrina smiled.

Hum* "Hello, Katrina." She said sliding into the hanger, "Did you get the items Jason needs?"

"I have them right here," Katrina said, holding up the bag.

The door opened up, and Jason limped out. Katrina ran up to his side and tried to hug him but he threw up his hands.

"WAIT," he yelled. "A kiss would be better, I'm really sore." She kissed his cheek.

Hum* "Now please take this man to your home. He needs plenty of rest and lots of fluids. Follow the instructions I gave you and he'll be better in the morning."

Katrina got a real confused look on her face, "Ok." Either Sheila was getting ready to spring a trick on her or....

"I'll explain when we get there." Jason added.

Hum* "You two have a good day and I'll talk to you later." And after they left, Sheila shut off the com chip transmitter to Jason herself.

****

Hawk walked out of a food store with a bag full of groceries. He had slipped out of the Hotel room earlier and let Veronica sleep in. He had a wild idea for tonight and wanted to pick up some things before heading back to her. His first step was a florist, who was going to deliver an assortment later to the hotel room. The ingredients he had in the bag were plans for a romantic dinner, it had been a while since he's cooked, but he was looking forward to it. He only needed one more item.

He entered Little Chicago with a spring in his step. There were about five customers in the club; four sitting at a table together, with travel packs, and one at the bar counter with a blue duffle bag. Hawk walked up behind the bar and approached Steve at the register.

"Hey, you still have some of that Kentucky Whiskey that you and Jason are always talking about?"

"Very few bottles left," Steve grunted, "Why?"

"I want one for a special night with Veronica tonight. Can I have one?"

Steve thought about it and then nodded his head, "Sure, why not, it's for a good cause."

Then someone yelling from the front door made both of them turn their heads.

"HEY GRUNT, REMEMBER THE DAVI!"

Steve turned and saw the blue bag sitting alone on the bar counter. "DOWN!" he yelled grabbing Hawk and pulling him to the ground.

The bag exploded.

****

Careese was gathering what was left of the inventory sheets from Kyler's office. "I hope this is all. I'm not trying to be vain but I think we did one hell of a job."

"I agree," Kyler answered.

"Well, I'm going to set this on Katrina's desk and leave early. I'm having dinner at her house tonight to meet this man of hers, so I'll see you tomorrow."

"Later," Kyler waved.

Careese walked down the hall carrying the inventory report and started humming a tune. She was looking forward to meeting Jason and was so happy that Katrina had finally found someone. As she rounded the corner into Katrina's office, her song stopped short when she saw a blue duffle bag sitting on her desk.

The bag exploded.

****

Veronica awoke lying on top of the bed covers. It got hot last night, in more ways than one, and she enjoyed the breeze blowing on her naked body. Suddenly she realized that something really warm was on her right-side hip and when she turned her head to look, she heard the purring. Hawk's trill was curled up on her side fast asleep. She cautiously reached down and rubbed its belly, and it purred louder.

Things were getting ready to change. She was going to have to notify the rest of the band that she was going to retire from the business. She wanted to stay with Hawk and build a future together. She now knew that because of true love, her dreams of having a family were closer than ever.

Hearing the door open in the other room, she moved out of bed slowly not to disturb the trill. She had a good rest last night and was ready to start another exciting day with the man she loved. She ran to the door, opened it and was startled to see a large husky man standing in the living room.

"Well, well, well, what do we have here?"

CHAPTER 15

Shattered wood and glass were everywhere. The air was filled with dust and debris making it very hard to see. The crackling of several fires ran throughout the club and was the only thing illuminating the place.

Hawk and Steve were on the floor behind the main ice bin of the bar. Its strong construction blocked most of the explosion from them, but some flying debris did make its way to them.

"Steve, STEVE!" yelled Hawk, "Are you alright?"

"Outside of a lot of shrapnel wounds and the ringing in my ears, I'm ok. Did you get a good look at the guy?"

Hawk stood up, several wounds bleeding on his arms from glass fragments, "Oh yeah, he's mine."

Hawk ran toward the wide opening in the wall next to the double entrance doors. A crowd was already building outside and Base patrol police were pulling up when he stepped out. He glared deep into the crowd as he looked left to right for the man. His photographic memory remembered every detail; his hair, his coat, his build even right down to the earring on his left ear. His eyes glanced quickly through the growing crowd until he saw the individual getting on one of the transport buses down the road on the right.

Hawk cut through the thick crowd as the bus started pulling away. His speed made people turn their heads as he whisked by, and it didn't take him long to catch up to the bus before it had a chance to turn onto the next block. When he reached the side of it, as it was turning right, he lunged toward the third window. His arms broke through the glass and grabbed the man sitting in the chair by the shoulders, and using his legs as leverage against the side of the bus, he then yanked the man out the window. They both tumbled onto the ground but Hawk regained his balance and was standing upright as the man spun around and pulled out a gun. His quick shot caught Hawk in the left shoulder but didn't affect his opponent's determination. Hawk's eyes started to sizzle as they turned red.

Through the screeching stop of the bus's tires, Hawk grabbed the gun from the man's hand and flung it away before he had the chance to get off another shot. Before the guy had a chance to lift a fist; Hawk hit him four times in the face. The man stumbled backwards behind the bus, apparent broken nose bleeding uncontrollably, and regained his balance. When the man started to charge toward Hawk, he was met with a kick from a right foot that sent him falling backwards past the end of the bus. That's when another bus going the opposite direction ran over him.

****

Katrina was sitting on her couch with Jason's head lying in her lap. She slowly ran her fingers through his hair thinking about how much she loved him. He was so tired and had been asleep for over a course, but he truly needed it.

Before he fell asleep, he told her everything that happened to him and Sheila's ordeal. She couldn't understand how a machine would be able to have emotions. Programmed responses would be easy but to feel them as well? Would she be able to really understand what love Jason and she had?

Hum* "Jason, honey wake up we have an emergency?"

Jason's eyes bolted open and he sat up quickly startling Katrina, "What? What is it?" he said groggily rubbing his eyes.

Hum* "Have Katrina turn on her port news grid."

Jason turned to Katrina, "Something going on, turn on your news Vid."

Katrina reached over and pushed the button on her side console.

"............... reports have been confirmed. Once again, several explosions have occurred all over the planet. All ground control to all flights has been lost. All tower controls in Kelly, Cosal, Stuart and

Serin bases has been destroyed. Several of the Preedom offices have also been reported as been bombed.........."

Katrina held her hand to her mouth in shock, "Oh my GOD, oh my God! I have to go to the tower and see if everyone is ok." She stood up to leave.

Hum* "Tell her there is nothing left of the tower. From what I scan there is no tower"

"Katrina," Jason said holding her hand, "Sheila says there is nothing left."

Katrina sat back down on the couch and started to cry.

"Honey," Jason said, "They may not have been there."

"No," Katrina said through her tears, "Today was final on the inventory, they had to be there. And if it wasn't for me taking a vacation, I could have been...." Her face froze in a blank stare at the thought.

".................no idea what has caused the explosions or who could be responsible. It can't be........... this just in.......... Another explosion has occurred at a club called Little Chicago. We have not confirmed...."

"Let's go," Jason said standing up and pulling on Katrina's hand.

****

The scene around the club was in chaos. Fire details were still trying to put the fire out and several emergency vehicles were blocking the area off. Medical teams had set up a mobile unit just to the right of the building. Several wounded people were being treated, mainly for shattered glass wounds.

Steve was sitting on a bench with several bandages wrapped around his legs and Hawk was standing next to him when Jason walked up with Katrina.

"What the hell happened?" Jason said

Steve turned his head and shook his head. "You're not going to believe this shit, but the Davi is back."

"What? The Davi died on Earth. How the hell could the Davi be here?"

"Whoever it is, they knew that we were here," Steve added. "We need to get to a place and figure this out."

"Agreed," Jason said turning toward Hawk, "Where's Veronica."

"She's at the Grand Gate."

Looking back at Steve, Jason continued, "Can you walk?"

"Shit." Steve exclaimed, "This is merely a flesh wound."

"Ok, let's all go to the Grand Gate and talk this over in the room. We have to find out what the hell is going on and with Sheila's help; we should be able to come up with an answer to all this madness."

They didn't talk much on the way toward the Hotel, but moved faster than usual. The entire port was in disarray over the explosions and a lot of people walking around seemed lost. You could see several vehicles circling around the port, most of them cargo ships, just trying to find a place to land.

Reaching the front of the hotel, several people were in the lounge area watching the large vid screens in the lobby. You could hear people chattering amongst themselves, a few people were crying. When they stepped into the elevator and the doors closed, an eerie quietness filled the air. Not even the music was playing.

When they reached the door to forty-one, Hawk used the key card and opened the door. They could hear sirens from the open window across the living room and the air inside was cool and chilly. That's when they noticed that a couple of chairs had been turned over.

"Roni?" yelled Hawk heading toward the kitchen on the right.

Steve saw something small in the center of the room in front of an over turned chair. "Hey," he pointed, "What the hell is that over there?"

They all walked toward the object and saw it was Hawk's trill. Its head had been crushed in and the body was distorted. Blood stained the carpet under it and was splattered all over the chair next to it.

"RONI!" yelled Hawk as he ran to the bedroom door and hit it so hard that the door broke off of its hinges and fell to the floor. He walked over it to step inside.

"NO!" he yelled getting everyone else's attention to run up to the shattered door frame. That's when Katrina screamed.

Lying on the bed, on her back nude, was Veronica. Her throat had been slit open and the bed was soaked in her blood. A blank stare came from her eyes and her face was chalky white. Hawk ran to her side and knelt down toward her grasping her cold hand in his.

Steve turned his head and looked at the wall toward the left and saw the warning. Tapping Jason to get his attention, Jason turned and saw it as well.

Written on the wall, in Veronica's blood were these words.

"Fear the Davi"

CHAPTER 16

Steve leaned against the sink in the bathroom and looked at the cuts and bruises on his face. It had been a very rough night. It took all three of them to get Hawk to Katrina's apartment, because he was in such a fury that nothing was going to control him. First, they let him destroy everything in Jason's room, in hopes that it would calm him down. The only thing they needed to do was to prevent him from leaving in his state of mind. After two hours and thirty-five minutes, Jason cornered him and talked him down. Steve and Katrina still did not know what he said, but it calmed Hawk down enough to get him to Katrina's apartment. After stepping inside her apartment, he lost control again.

First Katrina was told by Jason to go into her bedroom, lock the door, and call port police about Veronica. He told her to have them notify them as to where they would take the body and for any questions needed to be answered. Then he told her not to come back into the other room until they called her. The lock on the door might help but bracing it with something wouldn't be a bad idea either. It only took another half course before they let her out.

Now, with the night gone and no sleep, Steve looked deep into his eyes in the mirror. He could see that his pupils still held there wide opened appearance but the black eye he had on his left eye was starting to turn purple. In the mirror's reflection, he saw the bathroom door open up, and Jason limp up behind him

"And I thought the Klebits were bad," Jason said grabbing a wash cloth from the towel rack.

Steve's rasping laugh turned into a cough as he spit out blood in the sink. "Hey, what time is it?"

Jason lifted up his watch to look, "I don't know, my watch is busted."

Steve started laughing again, "Ya know, I've seen him this bad once before," he said washing his face with a wet towel, "remember at Tego when he lost all that money to that con artist?"

"Oh yeah," Jason said moving over toward the sink and filling up the basin with water, "I also remember what that guy looked like when he found him."

Both the men started laughing at the memory as Katrina walked in carrying two cups.

"Well, it's good to hear you can laugh after all of this," she said handing each of them a cup. "This has Turonka leaves in it. It's a healing herb."

"Thanks, little lady," Steve said grabbing the mug and taking a sip. The warm liquid stung his cut lip but soothed his throat on the way down.

Jason took his cup and looked at Katrina's black right eye. "You're getting one hell of a shiner, honey."

She walked up to the mirror and looked at her face. The last two rotations put a lot of creases on her. Between the no sleep and Hawk's condition, she looked worn out and even frazzled.

Jason leaned over the bowl and doused his hands into the cold water and splashed his face. "So, is he in the same condition?"

"He's still sitting on the couch, if that's what you mean," Katrina stated, "but I'm not getting any closer to him to see if he's breathing."

Jason dried off his face and then stepped back out of the bathroom. Katrina looked into the mirror again and closer to her eye.

"You're lucky that was only his elbow" Steve said, "his fist causes a hell of a lot more damage. But no need to worry, you're still an attractive lady."

She smiled and kissed him on the cheek and left the room. Steve glanced back into the mirror again smiling and then reached up to his front tooth. It was loose to his touch.

"Shit," he said to himself, "I'm starting to run out of body parts."

When Katrina walked into the living room, she saw that Jason was sitting on the couch next to Hawk talking to him. He was responding and very calm. When she walked up to him, she was still cautious but more concerned.

"Can I get you anything to drink, sweetie?"

Hawk turned his head and took note of Katrina's condition, "Aw, Katrina, I'm so sorry. I didn't mean to…"

Katrina put her hand up, "All forgotten, so, how about that drink?"

He shook his head yes and she went to the kitchen to get a cup.

"Are you alright?" Jason said.

"Yes," he answered as he saw Steve walking in to join them. "I'm in control now."

Hum* "Oh, how could I be so blind and stupid?"

Sheila's words in Jason's ear changed his expression. "What is it, Sheila?" He asked, while the others looked at him for her response.

Hum* "Sitting in a hanger bay across from me is the third wing of a Davi separator!"

****

It didn't take long to reach Sheila's hanger, in fact Hawk, with his speed, was waiting for the others to catch up. When they finally arrived, they all gathered into Sheila's bridge to hear what information she had. Jason and Katrina sat in the two chairs; Steve leaned against the left wall, and Hawk kept pacing. Out the window they all could see the Davi ship sitting in the hanger across from them.

Hum* "I've accessed all the data material from their control board and found out some interesting things. This was the ship that pursued us out of Earth's orbit before the explosion; I had lost its whereabouts after the blast and thought it was destroyed."

"If that's the third part of the Separator, where are the other two?" Steve asked.

Hum* "The other two were here, according to their logs, but have returned to a large vessel orbiting the planet right now. In fact, there are several ships orbiting the planet, every one of them large cargo carriers."

"I still don't understand all of this," Katrina exclaimed, "If the Davi were earth terrorists, what do they want in this system?"

Hum* "Good question, I wish I had the answer. According to the records, they have been planning this for years."

"What the hell?" Jason added.

Within the silence in the bridge, everyone's mind was working on different thoughts.

Steve started to show signs of irritation but didn't want to get Hawk all fired up again. Jason's mind wondered why in the world they would need to rebuild a terrorist regime again. Katrina was confused about the whole situation, how one day things were great and the next so tragic. Hawk was still pacing, and wanted revenge.

Hum* "Good, I found the information I was looking for." A large screen folded down out of Sheila's ceiling and turned on. "I found the identifications of the pilots."

The first picture was of a stocky man; large broad shoulders and with a full beard. Hawk pointed at the screen. "That's the guy who blew up Little Chicago!"

Steve nodded in agreement.

Hum* "Correct, Levin Boyer, the remains of his body match his stats. He was the pilot of the ship across from us."

The picture changed to another man, a little thinner than the other one.

Hum* "This is Carlz Bradley, pilot of the second wing. It shows that he reported back to the main ship."

Then a large husky man appeared on the screen. His face was unshaven with a large flat nose and teeth that looked half rotted.

Hum* "This is Wenzell Crevis; his Stats match the records of the man who entered the Grand Gate hotel."

With that comment, Hawk went back to pacing around the bridge, his breathing becoming heaver and heaver. Jason started to get out of the chair to calm him but Hawk waved him off. "I'm ok. I've just got to find this man!"

"We will." Jason added.

Hum* "Hold up, everyone, incoming message being sent to all news feeds."

The screen switched to the local news vid.

………Attention people of Largo. We, the Davi, are in charge. All incoming ships and outgoing vessels will now be controlled by us. Preedom is no longer in charge. All operational and financial control will run from our main vessel, the Duress. In keeping with our request, we order that the vessel known as "ZEUS" be turned over to us immediately. If you do not comply within the first rotation, more destruction will occur……

The bridge was silent, even Sheila couldn't come up with anything to say. Everyone had blank faces as they looked back and forth at each other hoping that someone had an answer.

Steve leaned over the front console and looked out the window. "I just got a crazy idea," he said turning around to face everyone, "Let's give them what they want."

CHAPTER 17

The battle cruiser "The Duress" held orbit just outside of Largo's atmosphere. Its large cylinder shape held many weapons ready to destroy any attempt to stop them. Its two wings were half the length of its body and the engines in the back contained four booster Rockets. Two hanger bays, one on each side, held several smaller ships within. The front of the vessel was surrounded by a large window; the location of the ships bridge.

The bridge held only four personnel although it could easily fit thirty. The large space in front of the window contained several consoles with blinking lights and screens. With two personnel seated to the right and two to the left, everything was controlled from this room. All ground and air control were received and processed through this point.

Pacing in front of the window was Carlz Bradley. He was worried that he didn't hear anything from Levis, although Wenzell had already reported back. The success of the mission was falling into place rather well and he hoped that everything would be completed by tomorrow. The only thing they needed was ZEUS.

The most advanced system on Earth and its years of collecting data in this system made it even more valuable. With Zeus in place, they could not only run everything more efficiently but their defenses would be impenetrable. The power that Zeus could give to the strength of Duress would be unimaginable.

Suddenly, one of the controllers turned to Carlz, "Sir, I'm receiving a report from Officer Boyer, says he has the package and is on route to us."

"Excellent," responded Carlz, "Have him take it into the docking bay."

"Yes sir."

On board the third Davi separator, Steve was in the cockpit piloting the ship toward the large cruiser in front of him. Standing next to him was Katrina nervously biting her nails. The plan sounded good, but dangerous. She reminded herself that she always wanted to get away from the boredom of the office and find adventure, but this was not her idea of it.

Slowly moving behind the Davi vessel, controlled in the containment field, was Sheila. On board her bridge, stood Jason and Hawk.

"Are you sure this transporter works?" Hawk asked.

Hum* "I've already used it once, but I don't know how much of a distance it has or what repercussions it could have on you."

"I was passed out when she used it on me," Jason added, "so I have no idea what to expect." The thought of the Klebits still weighed heavy on his mind.

Hum* "I have the locations of the two individuals. Hawk, I'll be transferring you onboard the Davi main separator bridge, that is where Wenzell is."

Hawk clenched his fists twice, crackling his knuckles as he did.

Hum* "Jason, Carlz is on the main bridge, I'll take you directly there."

Jason checked his seven sixteen in the holster on his side.

Hum* "and just remember, if anything happens, I'm pulling you out."

"Sheila," Jason said, "I'm not leaving there until they are both dead. This Davi has to end here and now!" He pointed toward the ground emphasizing his words.

Hum* "Understood," Sheila said as she locked onto their locations. "Are you both ready?"

They both nodded their head that they were ready.

A sizzling sound indicated that the transfer was complete.

****

Wenzell had a cigar in his mouth and appeared to be relaxing reading a news vid. All the reports that had been broadcast were about the explosions and nothing was mentioned about a murder at the Grand Gate. He smiled thinking about what he had done and the final enjoyment that he got out of her. He reached up and touched his right cheek, feeling the deep scratches she left on his face. They will probably leave scars for the rest of his life.

Suddenly a bright flash occurred on the bridge in front of him and a small boy appeared out of thin air. He staggered to get his balance but recovered quickly.

"Who the hell are you, asshole?" Wenzell said standing up.

Hawks' eyes started to sizzle and Wenzell could hear them. As his anger grew, Hawk's eyes burned to a bright red. He tilted his head down and clenched both fists.

"I'm the last person you will ever see."

****

Carlz stood looking out the window at the Davi ship towing ZEUS closer to the ship. His mind raced about the future strength of the Davi. With this unit, they could never be brought down.

A sudden flash behind him caught the entire bridge crew by surprise as a man appeared. He stumbled and fell up against the wall and then regained his posture fast enough to pull out his gun. Carlz reached for his gun as well but was too slow for the intruder and was shot down fast. The four remaining bridge crew members got out of their chairs and ran for the exit door.

Jason walked up to the man on the floor and pointed his gun at the man's head.

"God bless the United Nations," and pulled the trigger three times.

****

Katrina and Steve, on the Davi separator, stood impatiently waiting for Sheila to tell them what was going on. It had been several taps since she told them the transfer was done but nothing had been reported since. Katrina bit her nails even more.

Suddenly a flash of light occurred and Hawk appeared on the bridge. He stood there breathing heavily, his face was pale and his eyes were so bright red that they almost glowed. His arms were at his side and his fists were still clenched. Lots of blood dripped from his fists and puddled onto the deck.

"Hawk," Katrina said running to his side, "Are you ok?"

"Everything has been taken care of." He said calmly. He stood motionless as he looked up at the ceiling, "Rest in peace, my love."

Hawk then slowly walked up toward the front and sat into the pilot's chair.

****

Jason felt like the weight of many lives had been lifted from his shoulder. He turned from the dead body on the floor and looked out the window at the Davi vessel and Sheila floating behind it. They did it, the plan actually worked. This ridiculous feud that had lasted for almost a two decade had now come to an end.

Then, suddenly, words behind him startled him.

"You know, I always knew that it would end up this way."

Jason turned, and there stood Rodger Brooks.

CHAPTER 18

Rodger Brooks stood in the doorway of the bridge's entrance with a gun in his hand. He slowly stepped toward Jason, his posture very erect and his steps like royalty.

"Smart plan," he said getting closer to Jason, "but did you really think it would work?"

Jason's face wrinkled in confusion, "I can't believe that you joined the Davi? What is it that is so vital in this system that they would continue their terrorist acts?"

"You idiot," Rodger yelled, "I didn't JOIN the Davi, I've ALWAYS BEEN DAVI! I was planted in that facility to get all information I could about Zeus. Do you really think that our strong cell was in those mountains?" His question hung in the air like a thick cloud. "We were ready to attack the Zeus installation when the Planet blew!" He then signed toward the front window with a jerk from his head. "As for this system, if you haven't noticed, whoever controls Largo, controls the system! I can starve out anyone!"

Jason shook his head, "as I have already said, it's time for the Davi to end NOW!"

They both fired their weapons at each other. Rodger was hit in the shoulder and fell backwards against the closed door. Jason was hit in the chest and fell to the floor. Rodger gleamed inside, knowing that Jason was going to be a problem. Once Jason is dead, he would go after that idiot Steve and get rid of him too.

Rodger readied himself to shoot once again, but a bright light surrounded Jason, and then, he was gone.

Rodger held his hand up to his bleeding shoulder and smiled. He knew that he had delivered a fatal shot to Jason and it would only be a matter of time before he was dead. He walked over to a small puddle of blood that was on the deck where Jason had laid and he scrapped his shoe across it.

"Only one more to go and the United Nations are gone," he said under his breath.

A loud hum took over the bridges speaker system. Crackling noises emitted throughout the bridge's machinery as Rodger turned his attention toward the front window.

There, hanging just in front of the glass, was Sheila.

Hum* "YOU BASTARD!"

He had no time to move. A large charge of energy shot from her guns and toward the window. As it hit, splinters of glass shot throughout the room and fire engulfed the entire bridge. The last thing Rodger felt was all the glass piercing his body. The explosion engulfed the entire front end of the ship and worked its way down the halls. Within seconds the entire vessel was destroyed. Sheila slowly backed off from the ship when the engines ended in a blinding blast.

On the Davi vessel, no one saw the explosion, even though the ships course was thrown in disarray. Both Steve and Hawk were looking at Katrina on the floor cradling Jason's head on her lap. Blood was all over her hands.

"Honey," Katrina said crying, "speak to me, please."

Jason slowly opened his mouth, tried to speak, but blood splattered out instead. Little dots hit Katrina's face and she started crying even more. She pulled his head up against her chest and he raised his hand slowly up to her hair. She looked into his eyes and he whispered very softly,

"I will always love you." And with those words, his hand fell down to his side and Jason was gone.

Katrina screamed at the top of her lungs. "No! This can't be happening…. this can't be happening!"

A silence fell over the bridge as the blast out the window dispersed back into the darkness of space again.

A hum came across the bridge's speaker.

Hum* "Not if I can help it."

Steve and Hawk looked up toward the window and saw Sheila floating outside.

"Sheila," Hawk said, "One thing about emotions is to learn how to accept life...." He turned to Jason with tears in his eyes, "and death."

Hum* "You all better stepped away from his body before I do something drastic."

Hawk turned and looked at her out the window, enraged at her comment. "How dare you threaten me!" His rage started to build up again, "He's gone, damn it, you're just going to have to live with it!"

Katrina pulled his body closer to her, never wanting to let go.

Hum* "Katrina, get away from him NOW!"

Katrina's eyes, full of tears, looked up toward the window. "Sheila how could you? How can you act this way?" She cradled his head again, her tears falling on Jason's cheek. "Don't you feel the loss and how much it hurts?"

Hum* "No and I won't! Life is made by how an individual wants it! Life doesn't come automatically messed up! I WILL NOT ACCEPT IT! I WILL NOT ACCEPT IT!"

Katrina put her hands to her ears, "STOP IT! STOP IT!" She screamed.

Hum* "Step away from his body NOW" yelled a deep male voice.

Everyone froze.

Hum* "I SAID NOW!" yelled the male voice again.

Suddenly a blast of energy flew from Jason's body and knocked Steve and Hawk down to the floor. Katrina was then thrown from under Jason and up against the wall. They all had been electrocuted and everyone was stunned and unable to move.

Deep within Sheila's circuits many components started changing switches. Several sparks flew throughout her body as she realigned systems and components. Another switch connected to another and more sparks flew throughout her circuits. Her solar panels channeled all the energy stored and processed it.

Deep under Jason's ear the com unit started to sizzle. A green glow filled the unit and started to glow the back area of

Jason's head. His body started to shake uncontrollably across the floor, shooting out electrical bolts and charges.

Katrina watched in horror as Jason's body continued to convulse on the floor. She was huddled up next to Hawk, and they held tightly onto each other. Steve was on the floor by the front window, unable to move.

Then a large blast of energy, like an exploding electric transformer, shot from Jason's body and dissipated, knocking everyone again.

Then, everything was quiet.

Katrina could not take her eyes off of Jason. She saw how his body was tossed around like a doll and then pinned up against the other wall. He was lying face down and still motionless, except............

Jason's hand started to move. Then his arm slowly rose. Katrina, still weak in the knees, crawled over to him, pulling with all her might. Her tingling skin still felt the blast that Sheila had delivered. When she reached Jason, she rolled him over and saw a green glow around the corner of his eyes, which now were open. He started blinking and the glow disappeared.

"Jason," she said softly.

Jason started to blink faster as he slowly regained his surroundings. He turned his head and looked at Katrina. "Katrina," he whispered, "what happened?"

She didn't answer just grabbed onto him and hugged him so hard, he grunted. As tears of joy fell from her eyes, Hawk and Steve slowly stood up and walked over to them.

"Y-you were dead," Hawk said still not believing what he saw.

"Dead," Jason said confused. He looked at Katrina's blouse and saw all the blood on it. Then he remembered Rodger on the bridge and how they had shot at each other. He looked down and saw all the blood on his own shirt and touched his chest.

"But I feel fine now, just a little tired." he said blinking his eyes.

"You should be tired," Steve added, "The way you were bouncing all over the floor. I don't know how she did it but Sheila brought you back to life."

"Sheila?" Jason questioned.

"Yeah," Hawk commented, "and she threw one hell of a fit doing it."

Jason smiled. "Thanks, dear."

No answer.

"Sheila?" Jason said louder.

Still, no answer.

Hawk ran toward the front window and looked out.

"NO!" Hawk yelled, and then sat down roughly into the pilot's chair.

Jason, with the aid of Katrina, slowly stood up and walked toward the front, arm-in-arm. When they reached the window, they saw what caused Hawk's response.

There, floating and slowly spinning out of control, was Sheila. She tumbled end over end as she drifted further away from their ship. No lights, no movement, no glow.

Jason could hear Hawk taking short, fast breaths as he lightly touched his shoulder. "Let's get her towed back to the hanger," he said

No answer.

Jason noted that Hawk wasn't breathing fast anymore and it worried him. As he peered around to the front of Hawk's face, he saw that Hawk's eyes had turned completely black, no color was in them. He waved his hand in front of his Hawk's face as Steve walked up to the other side of the chair.

"Hawk," Jason said lightly shaking his shoulder. Still there was no response.

Steve reached over and laid his hand on Hawk's chest. "He's still breathing, but very long slow breaths." He then reached across the console and started pushing buttons. "I've got her," Steve said as he re engaged the towing beam on Sheila.

Within the next twenty taps, they soon found themselves landing in Serin base.

EPILOGUE

Sheila's body sat on the cold floor of hanger thirty-seven. She was tilted over on her right side and her outer hull didn't even glow anymore. To Jason, she looked cold.

Katrina was crying. She had lost her friends and now this tragic loss really hit her hard. Sheila was everything to Jason and she, too, grew very fond of her. She also saw that it was affecting Jason so hard that he couldn't take his eyes off of her. His eyes were glazed over and his face was pale.

She turned her attention toward Steve crawling out of the back end of Sheila's controls wiping his hands on his pants. He approached both of them shaking his head.

"Everything is burned out," Steve stated, "No tapes, no data, not even one lit unit. She's gone, Jason."

Jason swallowed hard.

"How's Hawk?" Katrina asked.

"This is the first time I've seen him like this," Steve answered. "So, we're going to have to ride it out and see what happens."

"Where do we go now?" Katrina asked looking toward Jason for an answer.

"Well, I still have my small apartment," Steve pointed out, "outside of that, nothing."

"I still have my apartment," Katrina smiled, "outside of that, I have my whole life ahead of me. Life is made by how......" Then she started to cry again.

Jason remained silent. All the changes that had happened in the last two hours still had him stunned. His conscience kept reminding him that Life was a forever changing and you had to make the best of what was handed to you. The best thing in his life was standing next to him, he reminded himself, so he needed to shake himself off and continue on.

Tell her how much you love her, his conscience said, let her know. Don't be so stubborn with your feelings.

"Katrina," he said turning toward her.

"Yes," she said through her tears.

"I... I..." he stuttered. He couldn't talk because everything still felt hazy, like a dream. He felt like he hadn't had enough sleep, and it all seemed fuzzy. His conscience within him even tried to comprehend. 'Snap out of it,' it told him. 'Can't you humans ever get to the point'...

Jason's expression became alarmed as he glanced back at the dead hull, "Sheila?"

Katrina grabbed the sides of his face gently and turned him back toward her. "Jason, she's gone, and I'm here, always."

A long tear ran down his cheek. He looked deep into her eyes and realized how much he loved her, how he almost never saw her again. He grabbed onto her and embraced her into a long passionate kiss. This was reality, a true dream that he hopes to never wake up from. He held her tight and felt the love burn between them. Her arms wrapped around him rubbing his back, gently and he became relaxed and at peace. The warming of their bodies increased their energy, and they felt renewed and fresh.

Jason released his lips from hers and whispered in her ear, "I love you very much, and will never, never leave your side."

She hugged him again, crying into his shoulder.

"Excuse me," Steve said tapping them both on the shoulder, "I really don't want to break this up, but I could use a shower and something to eat."

"Sounds good to me," Jason said smiling to Katrina as he wiped the tears from his eyes.

"Let's head over to my place," Katrina said letting out a sigh, "I've got plenty of food"

"How about some alcohol? I could use a drink as well," Steve added.

Katrina smiled, "I have plenty of that as well."

They all started walking away when Jason's conscience spoke again.

'Don't drink too much.'

He turned and quizzically stared at the blank ship behind them.

THE END?

The following is a sample chapter from the book "The Resurrection", Richard Crane's sequel to "The Sacrifice".

  Walking along the street was almost like a dream. The sun was just rising and everything had an odd look to it, making images not clear but rather fuzzy in appearance. A light mist filled the air and you could smell the odor of fresh water. It looked like a typical day in the port, but the noise level was low, almost nonexistent, and eerie. You could even hear the echoes of your own feet hitting the pavement and resounding off the solid walls around you. Slight sounds of dripping water, a brown beetle shrill, a wind gust, and even a person coughing down the street broke the silence but just gave a little notice to the stillness around. Another gust of wind just tried to make everything seem the same, just like nothing had ever changed.

  Then, stepping around the corner, the regular turned unfamiliar. The smell of burnt wood filled the air, clutter still was thrown about the street, and that regular walk turned into a frightening nightmare. The surrounding area was different; the brisk morning had turned into a chill down the spine, objects were not fuzzy but completely unrecognizable, and it seemed that the noises that were noticed before no longer existed. Nobody even coughed.

  Stopping at the entrance, emotions and images started taking control redirecting thoughts. The door didn't look that bad, in fact hardly touched, and even the lock still worked, but the windows had been blown out and were now covered with boards and police tape. The sign, that usually stayed lit above, was now dark and lifeless. The place used to hold lots of life, fun, and feelings of comfort, but now, it displayed the death that had surrounded everyone in the last twenty-four courses. Hurt, worn out, and barely holding its own, the building looked sad. It needed someone to breathe new life back into it and make it feel young again.

A sparkle of a key broke the dimness of the area as it was pulled out of a pocket and inserted into the lock. A hard twist to the right, and the lock clacked open, splitting the silence with a sound that shouldn't have been as loud as it was. It took a strong shove to open the door and it argued the motion with cracks and creaks as it was forced. By the time it was fully open, the echoes of its strain could be heard throughout the empty building.

Suddenly, a flashlight bulb split the darkness in the room and things became a lot clearer. The damage was substantial, but salvageable. But who would want to start it all over again and bring it back to life? Who was willing to find the time and money to bring back its glory? Could it ever be the same?

The light proceeded to wander toward the left where several stools still stood next to the bar. Reaching the counter, the person walking the flashlight turned it upward and set it upon the bar's surface. The reflection off the mirror and the ceiling illuminated more of the room giving another spooky feeling of death. No music played, no lights flashed, and shadows danced around the once active stage. A little sound of trickling water was the only apparent noise happily bouncing off of something metal.

Steve pulled out one of the chairs and sat down on it. It creaked but held firm. He let out a long sigh of relief and anguish, taking note that this all happened so quickly. He had spent the night at Katrina's apartment where Base Security talked to all three of them for about two courses and cleared up everything about the destruction, the deaths, and the outcome. After the Police left, they all got something to eat, and then Steve took a shower. When he returned to the room, Jason and Katrina were having a drink, and he joined them. They each had a couple, and then decided to call it a night. Not much was said, for they all were still traumatized from the events, but they soon ran out of energy and went to bed. Jason and Katrina slept in her room, and Steve slept on the couch. He had tossed and turned all night, and then realized that it was futile to sleep. He got up, got dressed, and walked to "Little Chicago" to clear his mind. That proved to be a mistake for the visions started running through his head again about the consequences leading up to this point.

At first there was the explosion here, then, the second explosion at the Tower. That was all followed by Veronica's death, Jason's death, Sheila's death, Jason's return, then last, Hawk's coma. Seven deaths total, on the ground, and many in the air. He had no idea how many people were on board Rodger's ship when Sheila blew it up, but they all deserved it, especially Rodger. Good riddance. The thought of even attempting to enforce Davi rule made him sick to his stomach.

He still couldn't figure out why Rodger got involved with the Davi in the first place, especially when he was from Tennessee. During his whole life, Rodger was a United Nations citizen and had a good upbringing. He was from a rich family, went to the best schools, and was given all the comforts of home. Everything that he stood for was the complete opposite that the Davi enforced. The United Nations stood for peaceful, non-controlling countries who had adopted a declaration to grant freedom and equality to all forms of life and needs. Poverty was a thing of the past and together they combined their knowledge to find cures for many diseases and provide food for the population. Cancer, hunger, diabetes, brain disorders, and even psychological disorders were long gone to the past. Hell, even the animal life on the planet had protection. Life became precious and the respect for others was just a natural fact. Racial discrimination was gone, animal cruelty was gone, and even money was gone. People were granted allowances per day for use and nobody profited off of the other. We all lived together as an equal and were happy.

Then, the Davi came. The Davi wanted to rule everything on Earth. They believed that their government was the answer to organized spiritual enlightenment. Anyone who did not join them, were marked as inferior and exterminated. They quickly gained control of land that was major energy sources for the planet and used its control for demands. Several countries were lost across the continent of Europe and were formed into either Davi supporters or massive grave yards. They had gained control of almost half of the

European continents and were establishing themselves as the only true race. Then, of course, the war dragged on for years. Steve enlisted to help fight and was a marine fighter on the ground. He had been through many battles and had the scars to prove it. After four years, he transferred to the air force to become a fighter pilot flyer. He went through the most heavily guarded runs and missions to where he had shot down many enemy targets. His size, skill, and victories gained him the nickname 'Badass of the sky'. When he was transferred to the station at Ford Base, he was assigned to drop the bomb. The bomb, in all hopes, would end the Davi occupation and take out the leaders. Taking out the world was not the plan. Nobody would have guessed the outcome.

It only took Zeus about twenty minutes to find Steve's OAJ, and another forty to get him onboard. After meeting Jason and Rodger, the three of them became determined to find a future. The star charts that Zeus contained gave the three of them possible destinations to pursue. They were only in space for six months and even then, they had plenty of supplies to last another three years if needed. The ship that Zeus was contained in had four sleeping compartments; each with its own bathroom, a kitchen, a pantry, and a large gathering room with plenty of electronic entertainment devices. Essentially, it was an apartment with no yard to upkeep. They kept themselves busy and with the information that Zeus contained, they would never run out of topics to learn. They had heard of individuals who had become 'Space Happy' on long deep space explorations, but at least they returned home. The three of them had no home to return to.

Steve sighed and turned his head toward the floor on the other side of the bar and something caught his eye. "Well, I'll be damned," he said out to nobody as he got up off the stool. He then grabbed the flash light and walked toward the end of the bar. He really didn't have as far to go as usual, because the end of the bar didn't exist anymore, for it was now in fragments all over the room. He stepped and crunched his way over broken glass and wood until he found himself at the object he had seen. He knelt down toward it and shined the flash light upon it.

The large safe under the counter didn't have a single scratch on it and it was still closed. He hooked the light under his left arm and with his right hand, started turning the combination lock to its numbers. After four turns, the door clicked, and Steve swung open the door. He crouched closer to the ground to get a better look and pointed the flash light into the large safes' contents. He was quite surprised what he saw.

None of the money was burnt, a lot of the building's assets were still intact, and glistening in the light were three bottles of Kentucky Whiskey. Not one of them was broken. He reached in and gently pulled one out.

"Hello, sweetie, nice to see you," he said as he twisted the cap and heard the seal crack upon opening. "This is going to feel good," he said as he lifted the top to his lips and took a slow sip. The liquid, even though it was cold, gave a warming sensation as it went down his throat. He then took a deep breath and slowly exhaled.

A scuffling sound came from the front entrance door, and Steve hurried to his feet to see what caused the noise. He took the flash light and aimed it into the direction of the disturbance and blindsided Jason right in the eyes. Jason quickly put his hands up to block the lights and cocked his head to the side. "Steve, is that you?"

Steve aimed the flash light down toward the floor and sat the bottle upon the countertop. "Yes, it's me. I couldn't sleep."

Jason smiled and walked toward the bar, "I thought that you would probably be here." His voice still sounded tired and weak. The past few courses had really taken its toll on him and it showed deeply in the lines in his face. The thought of him being dead earlier still felt like a dream and he couldn't shake the image. Of all the different stories that he had heard about death, feeling a calming serenity, seeing family that has passed before you, or even seeing a light, he remembered nothing. Maybe he wasn't dead long enough to experience it. Maybe the afterlife wasn't what it was believed to be. Maybe there was no afterlife. His thoughts drifted back to the present as he looked at Steve and noticed the silence of the room. "Are you ok?"

Steve pointed the light toward the bottle on the counter, "I will be after a couple of swigs of this."

The light bounced off and through the bottle at the same time and glimmer lines bounced off the walls. Particles danced through the room around the beams and lightly floated to destinations unknown.

Jason's eyes squinted and he got a better look at the object in the light, then he started to develop a slow grin across his face as the bottle became clearer. Memories started to fly through his mind as the past was brought back to him. Many times, were recalled; the relaxing nights, the quick sips, the party nights, the 'how the hell did I wind up on the garage floor' nights.

"Well, I'll be damned," he said as if repeating the echo of Steve's previous words. "Did any of the glasses survive?"

Steve turned the flash light back up the counter, "have a seat and I'll find out. If not, we can drink it straight out of the bottle." He turned and started looking through the debris around the holding area.

AUTHOR PAGE

Richard Crane Is the author of three books. He is a
veteran of the United States Navy and spends
most of his time watching movies, drawing, or
supporting his favorite sports team. He's a diehard
Science-fiction fan and also enjoys a good horror
movie. He's a collector of many movie items and
enjoys long walks with his dog. He currently lives
with his family in Central Illinois.

Other books by Richard Crane;

"Tainted"

"The Resurrection" (Sequel to "The Sacrifice")

"The Angel"

Author information

DO NOT PRINT

Brian Aymer

531 S Glenwood Ave.

Springfield Il. 62704

(217) 503-6341

darthbrimer@att.net

www.ingramcontent.com/pod-product-compliance
Lightning Source LLC
Chambersburg PA
CBHW031622040426
42452CB00007B/631